Nose Over Toes

by
Wendy Smith
With Barry, Matthew and Nikki

First published in Great Britain 2015

by

FOR THE RIGHT REASON

Copyright (c) 2015 Wendy Smith

A CIP catalogue record for this book is available from the British Library

ISBN 978-1-910205-71-6

Printed & Published
by For The Right Reasons
60 Grant Street, Inverness, IV3 8BS
fortherightreasons@rocketmail.com
Tel: 01463 718844 or 07717457247

INTRO

Matthew was trying so hard with his walking. His legs were painfully thin and looked too weak to support his weight but Matthew being Matthew just persevered and practised at every opportunity. Jan concentrated on teaching Matthew how to get up on his feet unaided.

"Nose over toes" was her much repeated instruction! With his usual grim determination he mastered this skill over a period of time but for you to get the full picture I need to explain how he managed to achieve it. First he got into a kneeling position. Once kneeling he got his right foot forward and putting his weight and balance through this he gritted his teeth and "launched" himself forward and upwards. To get upright might take many attempts but once he was up on his toes he had to keep moving as it was the momentum that kept him there! His momentum not always taking him where he wanted to go! Sometimes he just spun around on the spot before he could aim for his intended destination. As soon as he stopped moving down he went.

Saturday's Child

"Are you having a baby?"

To which the very quick reply was, "No we would like cod and chips twice please."

This was not a scene from Monty Python but the greeting and my husband's subsequent reply, to the young lady on door duty at Colchester Maternity Hospital. It was just turned midnight so it was now Saturday 1st November 1980 and it was to be the last wisecrack my husband Barry would make for a long time.

Before I tell you what happened after we passed through those doors I need to paint some background to our story.

CHAPTER 1

LIFE BEFORE MATTHEW

Barry and I have known each other since we were fourteen. He had arrived at my secondary school during the third year. Barry had managed to persuade his parents that, as the newly opened Catholic school he attended was not yet geared up for GCE examinations, he should become a pupil at the very old and established local school that I and most of his mates went to.

What a whoppa!!

The real truth is that our school had a very superior and successful football team which football crazy Barry was determined to be a part of! I cannot say that as Barry swaggered into our classroom that first morning it was love at first sight. He was obviously big headed and not over endowed with good looks.

I was by no means perfect, in fact when Barry asked the boys in our class about me he was told, "Forget it mate, she's the Lord Mayor's daughter!"

Of course I was no such thing, but like all 14-year-old girls my sights were set much higher than the immature boys of our own age!

Barry made the school football team as goalkeeper and then on into the North East Essex schoolboys' team. Heady heights indeed!

On our first and last date at fourteen he asked me if I was just going out with him because he was a famous footballer! Unprintable reply! We did however live in the same neighbourhood so soon we began walking to and from school together, sharing our textbooks and helping each other to revise for exams.

I wouldn't describe us as best friends, but we were part of the same crowd and always there for one another as agony aunt or shoulder to cry on whenever a

5

romance came to an end. If we found ourselves at a loose end there was always company around the corner!

I remember laughing at my sister when she asked why Barry and I weren't an item as we spent so much time together. What a joke! But finally we realised that maybe it wasn't such a bad idea! The Lord Mayor's daughter and the Famous Footballer have been together ever since!!

Barry came through the schoolboy ranks of football. After we left school he started a printing apprenticeship, which was mainly college based. He was extremely fortunate to get an apprenticeship, especially in printing, due to it being almost a closed shop at that time. I joined the Post Office and worked in Telephone Accounts for what was to become BT.

Then to Barry's delight Colchester United signed him on and he became a bona fide professional footballer, which then made me a WAG! Joining Colchester meant Barry had to leave his apprenticeship, a very big deal in those days, and Barry will always be eternally grateful to his Mum and Dad for agreeing to sign his release papers.

Being a Wag in those days was very different from today. We never wore designer clothes or got featured in Hello! Every home game we huddled together in our own exclusive part of the Layer Road stand and, if we were very lucky and the right steward was on duty, we had a cushion to sit on! Attending one home match against Reading I caused quite a stir when I won the "Golden Goal" competition with my ticket for the timing of the first goal of the game; a goal coincidentally conceded by Barry. We both got quite a ribbing over that but fortunately Colchester won the game 2-1.

As a local lad Barry was very well known, and during the close season he was frequently invited to open shops and summer fetes. One shop opening I remember with consummate embarrassment. A new furniture shop was opening in Colchester High St and Barry was invited to do the honours. He cut the tape and then we went inside to admire all the beautiful shiny furniture and rolls of carpet. As Barry started his little welcome speech I very stupidly leant against a roll of carpet and started a chain reaction, a domino of carpets. Oh the shame of it! Barry as quick as a flash asked the assembled party if they had heard of Frank Spencer as just for one day only he had brought Frank's sister along!

Barry's career at Colchester United was going well. The only downside was all the injuries. Goalkeepers in those days were not as protected as they are now and he was frequently kicked in the head. He was on first name terms with most of the doctors and nurses in the casualty department. I remember that several of our friends were getting married around this time, and although he couldn't make the actual ceremony he always tried to get back for the evening reception, very often arriving at the celebrations sporting stitches and hair slicked back with Vaseline over the wound. Very fetching!

He had a regular first team place and was attracting the attention of some big clubs and then disaster struck. During a training session he made a save which really hurt his wrist. For a few games he bravely carried on but the pain was getting worse and so he was despatched to see an Orthopaedic consultant. The doctor confirmed that he had broken the scaphoid bone and Barry's wrist was put in plaster for six weeks, not the best of news for a goalkeeper. It transpired that he had played some twenty games with a broken wrist. After six weeks the plaster came off but unfortunately the bone had still not healed; no doubt the delay in diagnosis of the injury had not helped matters. Whilst the plaster was still on Barry got septicaemia following an infected wound in his big toe! He nearly died and at one time it was deemed that he was too ill to be moved to hospital.

The next step with regard to the wrist injury was a visit to a Harley Street Consultant, who gave Barry three choices:

Have surgery to fix the bone in place: This would mean his wrist lost movement.

Wear a leather gauntlet; again he would lose flexibility in the wrist.

Leave things as they are and carry on playing with a broken wrist.

Barry decided to go with the third choice knowing his dreams of top-flight football were ended.

He did make the first team again but then was released by Colchester United and offered a trial with Bob Stokoe at Sunderland. Sunderland had just won the FA cup so it was a very exciting opportunity. It was also Barry's first time at living away from home, and for us to be apart. I became a regular rail traveller from Colchester to Sunderland.

Although he has great memories of his months with the club, there wasn't a real career opportunity for him and so he was released and given a transfer to Walsall.

In November 1973 he was made an offer by Weymouth FC. It was as a part time professional, but part of the deal was a rent free bungalow and the club would help him to find a job to go along with the football. No more long distance relationship for us! We had set a date for our wedding, June 22nd, but now we could bring it forward. Obviously, because of the football season, it would have to be a Sunday and so we decided on the 10th February, just a few weeks away.

CHAPTER 2

WEDDING PLANS!

Barry was a Catholic and so on a weekend home from Weymouth he made an appointment for us to visit our local priest to discuss our revised wedding plans. We went along on the Sunday afternoon and I have to say we didn't get the best of welcomes!

The priest was not at all impressed with what we had to say, firstly because I am not a Catholic and secondly because we had brought the date forward because of a bungalow! The priest was determined to make life as difficult as possible for us. One of the little Pearls he threw into the meeting was to ask Barry if he had considered marrying a good catholic girl, to which Barry replied that he'd yet to meet one.

As I was not a Catholic the priest insisted I receive "Instruction" from him. After Barry went back to Weymouth I agreed to see the priest after work on Monday. He took this as an opportunity to breathe hell fire and brimstone at me if I didn't agree to allow our future children to be brought up within the Catholic Church. I argued it would be for them to decide for themselves but my protestations were falling on closed ears.

We both reckoned without my dad, who banged on the door during my first session and very politely told the priest we had heard all that was required.

Undaunted, the priest then insisted on a copy of my Baptism certificate before I could be married in his church. This was a little more challenging as the church in which I was christened had suffered a fire and guess whose records had been destroyed! We did however, albeit in a race against time, manage to get a copy.

Barry's eldest brother Philip was a priest in Chingford and of course we wanted him to perform the ceremony. This I was told by the priest would require a special dispensation from the bishop. I rang Philip in a panic and with his help we managed to overcome this obstacle.

But the priest was not finished yet, for as we wanted to get married on a Sunday we needed a special licence. Philip to the rescue again! This special licence cost me a pound, for which Barry has yet to reimburse me. He tells me he will pay the money once he is sure he has had value for his money!

Finally, not to be outdone, the priest then announced during the eleven o'clock Mass on the morning of our wedding that Prayers for the sick would be held at 3 o'clock that afternoon the very time we were due to Wed. Ever had the feeling you weren't welcome? This did have Barry's Mum banging on the priest's door straight after mass.

Apart from the awful weather, for which I couldn't blame the priest, the day passed without further hitch. Just as a postscript: Weymouth's game against Yeovil on the Saturday was postponed because of snow.

CHAPTER 3

START OF MARRIED LIFE

Living in Weymouth was great fun. I had a job I really enjoyed at the Department of Health and Social Security. We made lots of new friends and had lovely times when our old friends came to visit for holidays and weekends.

The only problem being that Barry was unable to find a part time job to fit in with his football career. He worked for a few weeks as a builder's labourer, which was far from ideal. After this he worked six months for Tesco in charge of deliveries until Weymouth reached the first round proper of the FA cup against Peterborough away, then taking them to two replays before Peterborough eventually won. So he needed some extra time off, only to be told you either come in to work or go to Peterborough. Needless to say he chose the latter and was sacked.

Footballer's wages in those days even with appearance money and win bonuses do not compare to those of today. We really wanted to get on the property ladder and although we were having a lovely life financially we were just treading water not earning enough to save for a deposit or qualify for a mortgage. Barry threatened to walk out on the football club if no job came up and he did; with us doing a moonlight flit early one Sunday morning with Barry's brother Alan. He had hired a van and driven from Colchester down to Weymouth to bring us and all our possessions back to Colchester. We always laughed about this trip as due to people parking very close together, Alan did take a couple of wing mirrors off along the way!

Weymouth released Barry from his contract and we headed back to Essex. I returned to my old job with

British Telecom and, after a year as a milkman, Barry started his career as a Man from the Prudential.

In April 1975 we had our first mortgage on a three bedroom terraced house in Colchester. Barry signed for Clacton Town as a midfield player; he'd had enough of playing in goal. Life was peachy. We worked hard and played hard.

In the summer of '76 we moved to Alresford, a lovely village just outside Colchester. Our new house had an enormous garden, and was the scene for many wonderful parties and family gatherings. Bonfire night became an annual event for all our family and friends.

Traditionally Barry built an enormous bonfire, our nieces and nephews made guys and everyone contributed fireworks.

Sometimes the night would coincide with Halloween and then our house would be invaded by the children dressed up as witches and ghosts.

You couldn't of course have a bonfire and fireworks party without piping hot tomato soup, sausages and jacket potatoes. Grandma's legendary homemade fudge and toffee apples were always on the menu.

The food tasted so much better when enhanced by the smell of Roman Candles, Sparklers, Rockets, Catherine wheels and bonfire smoke! They were brilliant times; little did we dream then, just how special one such night would become.

I have now filled in some background to our life before Matthew made his entrance. For six years it was comfortable, fun, uncomplicated and we enjoyed lovely holidays, nice clothes, smart cars and a beautiful home. Our plans turned towards starting a family. I will be speaking about the family many times so perhaps they should be properly introduced. Family trees have always confused me so please forgive my very basic presentation;

BARRY'S TEAM

Mum Denise 1908 – 2007

Dad Harold 1910 – 1984

Brother Philip m Elisabeth Sept 1980

CHILDREN:
Mark born March 1981
Christopher born Sept1983

Brother Alan m Ann 1966

CHILDREN
Claire born May 1968
Kerry born May 1971
Jane born March 1974
Victoria born March 1977

Sister Pauline m Colin 1967
Children: Tim born June 1968
Sarah born August 1970

Our best friends were and still are: Cheryl, Alan, Jean and Roger.

WENDY'S TEAM

Mum Tiney 1910 -1991

Dad George 1910 –1992

Sister Jean m Peter1969

CHILDREN
Alvin born Oct 1970
Helen born Nov 1972

13

CHAPTER 4

WHAT A BIRTHDAY PRESENT!!

April 11th 1980 was my 27th birthday. I had made an appointment with my GP Dr Peter Snell because I hoped I might be pregnant! Dr Snell was a very kind, caring man who tried unsuccessfully to hide behind a fierce exterior! He was always very supportive, especially in the years ahead. He confirmed on that day that I was indeed pregnant and in his opinion the baby was due on the 15th November. He also proclaimed me to be 'orribly ealthy'.

We filled in all the relevant paperwork and, armed with a prescription for the inevitable iron tablets, I stepped back into the waiting room to recover my husband. Slightly dazed but bursting with excitement, we couldn't wait to share our news with family and friends. Keeping the news to myself that afternoon in the office was torture.

After work we broke the news to our parents and the rest of our families. Everyone was thrilled with our announcement. It was news they had waited six years to hear.

My pregnancy proceeded without any problems. I felt really well and full of energy. Each month that passed I continued to be described as 'orribly ealthy' by Dr Snell. Oh yes I did have a touch of sciatica and was advised by Sister Smith at the surgery that the best cure for this was to get down on all fours and wash the kitchen floor, giving my bum a good wiggle as I went!

She was absolutely right and there was not a cleaner floor in Alresford. No morning sickness nor heartburn. How lucky was I!

I did have two cravings, Christmas cake with all the trimmings washed down with a pint of lemonade!

Barry's mum was kept very busy that summer baking cakes to keep me satisfied and I still love both.

Before I continue I must remind you that I am not a Catholic, and if my views offend I apologise but I relate the following story as I saw it and only include it as it happened during my pregnancy.

When Barry's brother Philip was a priest, Mondays were his day off. Every Monday he came home, maybe to work in the garden or to play a round of golf. His mother Denise always cooked a fabulous lunch to which Barry and I were invited. I was the envy of the office when I described what had been on the menu each week.

This particular Monday Barry came to pick me up as usual and told me that Philip had an announcement to make. We arrived at his parent's home where Harold and Denise both looked very strained, whilst Philip was wearing a grin from ear to ear. He told us he was giving up the Priesthood and was getting married to Elisabeth. Elisabeth we knew was a parishioner and also his hairdresser. The second wave of news was that they weren't far behind us and that they were expecting a baby in March.

For my part the hug and congratulations I gave Philip were warm and very sincere. At that time I had no idea of the emotional storm brewing. Being a non-Catholic it all seemed perfectly straightforward and natural to me. Philip had met somebody, fallen in love and conceived a child. They were to be married. Simple! How wrong could I have been?

The ramifications within the church were swift, ridiculous and hypocritical.

Basically if Philip were to give up Elisabeth and all thoughts of becoming a father to their child he could continue to be Father Philip, the priest with all blessing. The church would take care of Elisabeth and the baby.

Their future would be secure and comfortable with the child receiving the best possible education!

All embarrassment and scandal swept nicely under the Catholic carpet, the alternative was excommunication for both of them.

The shock and the shame to Barry's parents was heart breaking to witness. To have a son enter the Priesthood is a coup de grace; your religious 'street cred' overflows and so when it goes wrong the humiliation is very public and worthy of much "Christian" gossip.

Philip had chosen Elisabeth and had left his parish to come back to Colchester and live with his parents. After some discussion it was agreed Elisabeth should stay with us. This gave everyone time and space to come to terms with this new state of affairs and, more importantly, enable Philip and Elisabeth to make plans for their future.

Philip's first priority was to find a job and then get married. It all sounds easy on paper, but when their story was leaked to the newspapers all Hell broke loose. The story made headlines and the lengths the tabloids stooped to in order to get the story were horrible. Alan and his wife Ann were horrified to discover that, as their daughters were leaving school, they were confronted by members of the Press.

Harold and Denise's house was besieged, and I will never forget the press chasing Philip when he arrived home from work one evening, the photographer hanging out of the car as it took the corner on two wheels. Finally the Sunday Mirror caught him and forced him to stop. They told him that if he gave them an interview and a photo the other papers would back off. So he gave them what they wanted and they of course were lying; the banner headline to their article allegedly quoting Philip; ran "Ours is not a sex and sin relationship". For a while it was hot news and then, as with all titillation, it became yesterday's chip wrap.

Fortunately the press never discovered Elisabeth's whereabouts. This was in no small way down to my dad. George really entered into the spirit of keeping Elisabeth safe from the press. He took on the role of decoy, turning up at Harold and Denise's house, racing in, then out again. Taking off at speed the Press, thinking he must be on a mission, gave chase. Dad then treated them to a tour of the Essex countryside whilst back at home Philip and Elisabeth could come and go as they pleased!

The furore calmed down and life returned to almost normal. Philip and Elisabeth were married in September.

I finished work at BT in late September and became a lady of leisure, well on Maternity Leave. Harold papered the nursery for us with very lively woodland animal wallpaper. The main scene of the wallpaper was Mrs Badger's underground sweet shop; but more about that later!

Barry painted some Disney characters on one wall, Mickey Mouse, Dumbo and Joe Crow. At this precise time he was suffering very badly with toothache. It was so bad that sleep evaded him, but the painting helped to take his mind off the pain. Had his head been in the right place he might have painted his creations onto a board for future posterity, and not straight onto the emulsioned wall! What a discovery for future owners of the property.

We had planned to have our traditional Bonfire party on Saturday 1st November, as we thought the following weekend too close to the baby's arrival.

My sister Jean and her family came down from Hull for the celebrations. Jean and Peter stayed with us whilst Alvin and Helen stayed with my mum and dad. Friday October 31st was a really gorgeous Autumn day.

Barry went to play golf and Jean and family went out for the day with mum and dad.

I had an appointment with Dr Snell early that morning when he told me once again I was in the rudest of health, but advised me to put my feet up as much as possible whilst I still had the chance! After lunching at Harold and Denise's I went home and, taking Dr Snell's advice, put my feet up and read Daphne du Maurier's Frenchman's Creek.

Later that evening Jean, Peter, Barry and I spent a couple of hours in our local. We walked home around 11pm and I got ready for bed. Just as I was getting into bed my waters broke. I rang the Maternity hospital and was told to come in straight away. We knocked on Jean and Peter's door to let them know what was happening, picked up my suitcase and headed for Colchester.

Listening to the radio on the way we both burst out laughing when Blondie's "Tide is High" came on the radio.

We arrived at the hospital just after midnight, and a young lady answered our knock on the door. She was wearing a long plastic apron and very thick jam jar bottom glasses. We laughed about her that night because she reminded us of Olive, a character from a TV sitcom at the time called "On the buses".

She asked, "Are you having a baby?"

Barry replied "No we would like cod and chips twice please".

Her comeback was "Messy business having babies!"

Was she a latent spirit from Halloween? No, I promise you she was for real and, as I said at the start of the book, it was the last wisecrack Barry made for a long time.

CHAPTER 5

MATT'S ARRIVAL

Once through the Maternity Home doors this same young lady informed us again that it was a "Messy business having babies."

The following hours passed. All the usual procedures for those days were carried out, enema, shower and internal examinations but, apart from a few mild contractions, nothing much was happening. Barry was dispatched home to get some sleep with the promise he would get a phone call if anything changed.

As we were having the traditional bonfire party that night he also had a long list of "to do's" from me.

Barry returned to the hospital around midday and my labour was still not progressing. A doctor arrived from our GP surgery (Dr Snell was away on holiday).

This doctor advised me that as it was now over twelve hours since my waters had broken we needed to move the labour along. I was transferred to the wing of the hospital that catered for more complicated deliveries. Neither of us was unduly concerned as this was our first child and, apart from the discomfort of the internal examinations, I was feeling fine. Barry assured me all was organised at home. It was a minor detail that the host and hostess wouldn't be there but we had other things on our mind!

A foetal heart monitor was attached to me and I was hooked up to a drip. A young staff nurse told us the monitor was misbehaving: it had apparently been playing up all week.

The hours ticked by with my contractions becoming stronger but I was not "dilating". I was offered pain relief but as I was coping I refused.

By about 5pm we noticed the baby's heartbeat disappearing from the monitor every so often. We voiced our concerns and after that a staff nurse became a permanent fixture at my bedside. She chatted calmly enough but her eyes hardly left the monitor, with her face showing concern.

The Registrar on duty again offered me pain relief and again I refused. He told me "We don't give medals for bravery in this hospital" Both he, the Sister and a young House doctor were giving me internal examinations about every hour. It seemed an endless round of gloves and discomfort. Barry was sent out during these exams and each time he returned I was becoming more distressed. His concern for me and the baby was growing.

We were both by now very aware of the whispered conversations between the doctors and nursing staff.

Around 7pm the staff nurse reluctantly went off duty. Before she left she said "If you want to make anything of this please speak to me later". As I was now in great pain and very frightened her words were of little concern to us, but they were to return and haunt me.

At around 7.45pm the Registrar told us very dispassionately that the baby was not happy inside me and so they needed to perform an emergency caesarean section. Once these words were spoken the sense of urgency and panic was tangible. Barry was pushed out of the room as I was unhooked from the drip and monitor. I remember being transferred onto a trolley and rushed to the operating theatre

At some point on this journey I was aware of Barry running alongside the trolley. He said "Bye darling, I love you; Matthew if it's a boy Abbi if it's a girl!"

The theatre lights were dazzling above the operating table. The sound of the surgical instruments being prepared was deafening. A sea of green gowns and masked faces looked down on me as I was transferred onto the table.

They were talking to me but the masks muffled their voices and the panic enclosed us all. It is a scene I can recall with reluctant clarity and one that has invaded many dreams since, giving them nightmare status.

Then amid the panic, silence and gradually a distant voice calling my name, I'm struggling to wake up and comprehend what the voice is saying. I'm concentrating so hard: it's Barry's voice.

"Well done darling we have a boy, we have our Matthew, I love you, see you later go back to sleep now" Very happy to oblige I did! The time was around 8.30pm.

Since saying goodbye to me, and up until this present time, Barry was living the nightmare the day had become. There was not a waiting room for expectant fathers and so, as I was being taken to theatre, Barry went and sat in the window recess of the staircase. He was startled after a few minutes by a very tall man in green scrubs, obviously in a great hurry, taking the stairs two steps at a time. We now know this was the anaesthetist summoned from another hospital because there wasn't an anaesthetist present at the maternity hospital. It later transpired the anaesthetist's skills were being shared with the County hospital down the road, and at my hour of need he was actually performing an Appendectomy, so I had to wait until a relief arrived for him!!

This fact proved to be extremely crucial in the years ahead.

Matthew was born at 8.15pm and admitted to the Special Care Baby Unit at 9pm. Barry first saw him as a tiny bundle connected to lots of wires inside an incubator at about 10pm. Barry was told Matthew's condition was serious, but in our ignorance he believed all Matthew needed was a little oxygen and then he would be fine.

They had also explained to Barry that the cord had been tightly wrapped around Matthew's neck and that he had to be resuscitated as soon as possible. Barry left the hospital at about 10.30pm.

Back at home everyone was so excited and anxiously waiting for news. After his phone call the bonfire party had become even more of a celebration! Jean and Cheryl had done a fantastic job with the food while the beer and wine had flowed. Barry was ribbed mercilessly about the lengths people will go to save money on phone calls!

Harold, determined the new dad should get some sleep, poured him a very large whiskey or three. Denise, although absolutely thrilled, was privately very worried when Barry related the evening's events. For many years she had worked as a nurse in a hospital for children and adults suffering with mental and physical disabilities.

Back at the hospital I can remember waking up on Sunday morning to a man accompanied by a small child both standing beside my bed. The man introduced himself as Dr Symons the paediatrician. He asked if I was the young lady who had the emergency caesarean the night before. After saying I was he commented that this was hard to believe as I seemed so wide-awake. He told me Matthew had been resuscitated at birth and was undoubtedly brain damaged but to what extent only time would tell and then he left.

I should have been devastated but the simple truth is I was unable to comprehend what I had just been told. Alone and recovering from general anesthetic the words "brain damage" kept going round in my head, but I was unable to make any connection with the here and now, let alone what the future may hold. All I knew then was how desperate I was for Barry to get back to the hospital and to see my baby.

Barry arrived at about 10.00am and wheeled me down to the Special Care Baby Unit. My first thought when I saw Matthew was how much like my mum he looked! It was both scary and lovely to hold him.

A little tube came down from his nose and the nurses explained that this was a feeding tube which would only be used until he got stronger.

Sister Castle and Sister Bell, in charge of SCBU, were fearsome but absolutely lovely. They gave us so much support and confidence. Very kindly they allowed Jean and Peter in to see Matthew. Peter was a nurse and as they had to get back to Hull that afternoon the visiting rules were bent a little. The two Sisters described Matthew as having a bad headache and his condition as "irritable". Even after telling Barry what Dr Symons had told me about brain damage we were unaware of the severity of Matthew's condition. Sisters Bell and Castle told us what Matthew needed most right now was lots of TLC.

The next few days were interspersed with dramas surrounding Matthew's health. On the evening of 3rd November Sister Castle told Barry that Matthew was suffering from such a severe headache it necessitated a massive dose of Phenobarbitone.

Matthew was giving the staff great concern and the drug had been a "kill or cure" remedy. During this time I was confined to bed as I was severely anaemic and had to have a blood transfusion, so the graveness of Matthew's condition was kept from me. Thankfully the medication and skill of the staff in SCBU worked and he pulled through. Matthew's own fighting spirit had also revealed itself. By the 6th November he was well enough to come and visit me and the very first photographs were taken. The family album had begun!

Matthew was making such good progress by the 8th November he was discharged from SCBU and moved into a cot beside my bed.

I remember very well that first night of having Matthew beside me as he awoke crying in the early hours. After I had fed him, accompanied by the very loud and open-mouthed snores from the lady in the next bed, I then changed him. As I took his nappy off a projectile wee hit the wall and mirror beside his cot! Helpless with laughter I was very grateful his cot was not on the other side, my companion would have got a soaking! Two days later we were both allowed home.

CHAPTER 6

COMING TO TERMS

Taking a new baby home is a very scary experience. It is the realisation your life will never be the same again. The fears and questions start "How will I cope?" "What if he won't stop crying?" "Will I know if he is too hot/cold?" "Supposing he won't feed or drink properly". And of course the big one "Are we really ready to be parents?"

My fears were groundless. Matthew was a very contented baby. He fed and slept well. Of course he cried, especially when he had 3-month colic but even with this he was easily pacified. As his character was developing he became more engaging, so much so that people around us started voicing their doubts regarding the "brain damage". They made remarks such as "But he is so alert" "He watches every move you make" "Look how strong his little legs are, how he kicks and holds his arms up".

This last but frequent remark was very prophetic. It was so comforting to hear all this positive comment and we started to believe the brain damage had only been temporary.

At three months old Matthew had his first outpatient appointment with the Paediatrician. Dr Woodd-Walker had seen Matthew many times whilst he was in SCBU. Barry and I told him how well we felt Matthew was progressing and expressed the doubts we were having regarding his condition. We were willing the doctor to tell us that all was now well with Matthew.

If it wasn't we needed to know what the condition was called and what the prognosis was. (Highlighting our own ignorance, and human nature being what it is, our need for a label before we can accept or understand).

Dr Woodd-Walker looked us straight in the eye and told us that in his opinion Matthew had moderate Athetoid cerebral palsy. He explained this affected every muscle in Matthew's body, and that our baby would benefit from physiotherapy, starting as soon as possible.

He also told us that if we wanted to join a suitable club it should be the Spastics Society.

We would be going to see Dr Woodd-Walker in his very busy Baby Clinic every three months. The merry go round that was to become our way of life had begun. I recall going to the library and getting all the information I could on Athetoid Cerebral palsy. It was bewildering.

BARRY'S EARLY MEMORIES:

After the initial shock surrounding Matt's birth both Wendy and I realised that we couldn't just wallow in despair and self pity. We have always been quite strong minded people and from the early days of our marriage supported each other.

Once the possible extent of Matt's injuries was becoming apparent to us we started to dread friends, workmates and acquaintances making the comment "Bet he's going to be a good footballer like his Dad."

To a certain extent we had tried to spare people from feeling embarrassed by not saying anything about Matt's 'condition' but this rebounded on us at a later date when the severity of his disability became apparent.

One thing also has always remained ingrained in my memory. When still a young apprentice professional footballer I used to get involved with various charities and such like. One of the activities we actually did was to go to a Spastics Society centre in Kelvedon, Essex, called Drummonds, where we played wheelchair football with some of the patients. I subsequently adopted the Spastics Society as the charity that I wanted to support and always donated funds to them. What an irony! I never dreamt that Cerebral Palsy would have such a massive effect on my life in the future!

Matthew had his first physiotherapy appointment when he was five months old. To get into the Physiotherapy department you had to pass by a Reception hatch that was always closed. On every appointment however, as if by magic,the hatch would open and out popped a small head with darting eyes, demanding to know if we had an appointment. It always struck us as so funny, we even tried creeping down the corridor to try and get past her, but we never managed to. Barry and I nicknamed her "Hissing Sid" after the character in the Captain Beaky song.

Jean Ward the paediatric physiotherapist in whose care we were placed, confessed that Matthew was her first baby patient.

She had worked extensively with children suffering from CP and had also worked at Cheyne Walk in London. Her warmth and enthusiasm filled us with confidence. She explained so much more than any book could. Matthew had Athetoid CP and every muscle in his body was affected, some more so than others. The part of his brain that controlled all his motor movements was the damaged part, and so messages sent from here were not getting through to his limbs and muscles. Worse than that, the messages were getting mixed which caused movements he didn't want. These unwanted movements are called "involuntary movements" and they are going to make Matthew's life painful, frustrating, challenging and embarrassing.

His little body frequently went into spasm and really tightened, so our job then with exercises was to make other parts of Matthew's brain take over some of his movement control. We had to keep his little body stretched and flexible.

That engaging little thing he was doing with his legs and arms, mentioned previously, is a tell tale sign of CP. Jean described it as a primitive startle reflex and a definite "no no". Here I must confess to falling at the first fence. Even now, after twenty-seven years, when Matthew is startled his hands shoot up and he is very likely to fall over. Sorry Matt, bad mother again! Back to Jean, who showed us a range of exercises to do with him.

What Matthew had no control over was arching backwards with his arms and hands either side of his head. His head was mostly turned to one side and his legs almost continually "cycling". All of these cute little actions were compounding his condition and putting problems in the bank for later years.

His first exercises then were all about breaking these patterns and encouraging Matthew's body to come forward. He was unable to lift his head so Jean showed us how to lay him over a "roll" with his hands held on the floor, and then a motivator held above his head to encourage him to look up.

All of the exercises shown to us by Jean were faithfully carried out at home. I made a roll from an empty fabric tube which I then wound towels around. Jean came up with more ideas on improvising everyday items to use with his exercises, but we drew the line at using empty bleach bottles as leg splints!

Every night before his bath we went through his exercises. Matthew loved this time of his day and physiotherapy became an accepted part of his daily routine.

Harold's wallpaper also came into its own and became a very much-loved part of Matt's bedtime routine. As I mentioned before, the main scene was Mrs Badger's underground sweet shop depicting rows of sweet jars and candy canes. There were several staircases coming down to the shop with all manner of woodland animals making their way to the sweets. I would make up stories about the characters and Matt would follow my finger down the paper as the stories unfolded. As Matt got older the walls became a regular tool for his speech therapy. It was also a personal challenge, whenever he was put to bed by someone else, to come up with better stories than his Mum!

I hasten to add that in addition to talking to the walls that Matt also had books read to him.

Incidentally, of the Disney characters that Barry had painted on Matthew's bedroom wall, Joe Crow was undoubtedly Matthew's favourite and so was always given a special bedtime wave. Over the years folk have said to us that Matthew couldn't do what he does today if it wasn't for all the effort we put in when he was young. This may be fair comment to a certain extent but what is absolutely undeniable is that we were able to achieve so much with him because of Matthew himself. Had Matthew not been the type of easy-going child he was, our efforts would have been fruitless. Unless he was feeling poorly he co-operated and enjoyed everything we did.

From a very early age one word can sum Matthew up: "DETERMINED!"

Sometimes when faced with a situation they don't understand people will unwittingly make a ridiculous comment. It has happened to all of us at some time. The one we heard the most and still *is* guaranteed to make our toes curl is the classic, "These children are only sent to special people".

Take it from us they are not and we aren't!

CHAPTER 7

WATER BABY

My dad's sister Auntie Rene worked for the Army as a Pool attendant at the garrison swimming pool. When my dad updated her on Matthew's condition she was anxious to help. The Army physiotherapist, Major Tony Windsor, held an early morning session at the pool from Monday to Friday. Most of his patients were elderly, some were recovering from surgery or just enjoying the benefits of swimming in lovely warm water for problems such as arthritis.

Rene spoke to Major Windsor and told him all about Matthew and he agreed we could join this session. Major Windsor had recently become a father himself to a daughter named Helen. She was obviously the apple of his eye and he was delighted to talk about her. We had no idea that Helen was to play a large part in Matthew's teenage life.

Back to the pool. Major Windsor suggested exercises for us to do in the water with Matthew. He made a variety of floats to give Matthew maximum freedom and buoyancy to enjoy the water. To say Matthew enjoyed these times is an enormous understatement. He splashed, kicked and squealed with pleasure. There was never any shortage of willing arms to hold and play with him.

Rene was at every session and made it her job to get him ready for his swim and then dried and dressed afterwards. This enabled me to get ready and I know how much she enjoyed showing Matthew off to her friends and colleagues. In those days I didn't have a car of my own and so, on the days Barry was unable to take us, we had to rely on family or friend volunteers.

Fortunately there was never any shortage of those because everyone loved to watch Matthew becoming a water baby. It was probably at this time that we realised just how lucky we were to have such supportive family and friends. Without their practical and emotional support many a time we may have crumbled into self pity.

Sadly, due to economic cuts the temperature of the water at the pool had to be reduced and it was then too cold for Matthew. So after about a year our daily swim had to come to an end. We will always be grateful for the pleasure and benefit of water this gave Matthew, and for the kindness shown to us by Major Windsor and his early morning patients.

CHAPTER 8

ESTABLISHING A PATTERN OF LIFE

At a routine appointment with Dr Woodd-Walker we asked him what he thought Matthew's prognosis was.

He said that, in his opinion he didn't think Matthew would ever walk or talk, but without a crystal ball only time would tell. Hard words but the right ones to make me determined to prove him so very wrong! Matthew was now fourteen months old and, although he could make some sounds, he mainly communicated by eye pointing so Dr Woodd-Walker suggested we see a Speech Therapist.

We were introduced to Jackie Stubbs and she agreed that with the range of sounds Matthew could make we could possibly channel and develop these sounds into discernible speech.

The muscles in his throat were affected by his CP which explained his constant dribbling. His "gag reflex" was on the front of his tongue so he was extremely sensitive with lumpy foods. Jackie explained we needed to try and de-sensitise this to maximize Matthew's chances of achieving the mechanics of speech. Jackie told us the best way was to persevere with lumpy food, alarming though it sounded sometimes.

Jackie also recommended a "back up" system of communication to reduce the inevitable frustrations. Makaton, or any form of sign language, was impractical because of Matthew's poor hand control and involuntary movements and so she suggested "Bliss". Bliss was a labelling system for everyday objects and needs. Every object or word was given a symbol. As the symbols were learnt they were transferred onto a board. We put Bliss symbols on everything around the home and Matthew was a very quick learner. He did however become a victim of his own success, as obviously the more words you learnt the smaller they had to be on your board, and with his impaired hand control we came back to the beginning again.

It did encourage him to try and form the words and, coupled with tolerating larger morsels of food to chew and swallow, he was making great progress. Jackie came up with some ingenious ways to motivate and encourage Matthew to talk.

In the Speech therapy department there was a large sand pit but instead of sand it was filled with polystyrene chips. At the end of each session Jackie would hide toy cars in the pit and Matthew would do anything she asked of him in order to dive into the pit and find them.

Toy cars and vehicles were Matthew's favourite, so sometimes for his "homework" Jackie drew large pictures of maybe a fire engine; she then divided the picture into squares. In each square was a letter or sound and as Matthew attempted to make the sound the square was coloured in.

Mouth and tongue exercises, such as blowing silky scarves and bubbles (very hard to do with CP) were very important. Putting sugar strands around his lips and getting Matthew to try to lick them off with his tongue was another favourite. Drinking from a straw was a huge milestone.

Every 4-6 months Jackie gave Matthew a comprehension test. From memory I think it was called Renealle (sic). The results of these tests revealed consistently that Matthew's comprehension was well above average. We continued with the exercises and work on the Bliss board, which leads me to a little anecdote.

Our very good friends Jean and Roger have beautiful twin daughters, Katy and Jo, who are a bit younger than Matthew. Katy had to go into hospital for some minor surgery. In the bed opposite was a little lad with CP. This little lad was very distressed one day and the nurses couldn't understand why. Jean went over and beside his bed was a Bliss board. As soon as Jean explained to the nurses what the board was and how to use it, problem solved and smiles restored.

So the pattern of life for the next four years was established. Each week hospital visits for alternatively Speech or Physiotherapy and exercises from these therapies carried out at home on a daily basis.

BARRY

The early years after Matt's arrival were very tough for Wendy and me. A huge burden fell on Wendy because I had to carry on with my job at the Prudential. She was definitely the "main battler" for sorting out things for Matt, although I was affected in different ways! My promotions within the company were restricted geographically, as moving away was impossible because of the help and support we received from family and friends with numerous aspects of Matt's life.

I had been a member of Stoke by Nayland Golf Club for the two years before Matt's arrival, but ceased playing once we realized just how many appointments would be needed. There were regular special baby clinics to attend and ongoing physiotherapy and speech therapy sessions, to name just a few calls on our time.

Another pattern also revealed itself; we noticed every year around his Birthday, Matthew caught a cold.

Nothing particularly remarkable in that, but one night I heard what I thought was a dog barking in Matthew's bedroom. When I went to investigate, I discovered the "barking" was Matthew coughing and struggling for breath! It was very frightening. I rang our GP and was told a doctor would come at once.

Ordinarily we would have gone straight to casualty, but we knew there was an outbreak of whooping cough in the hospital. Contact with this disease would be extremely dangerous for Matthew. He had been unable to have the vaccination because of his breathing problems. Barry went to the top of our drive to look out for the doctor. Dr Lamont showed up in a squeal of brakes and a red three litre Ford Capri! He took one look at Matthew and said; "Up to the bathroom and let's get some steam going fast!"

Matthew had croup. Croup is caused by the muscles in the throat becoming swollen; the steam reduces the swelling enabling the patient to draw breath again. It sounds terrifying, but fortunately the steam works like a charm. Over the years I became an expert at working up a steam! Many times around his birthday Matthew and I spent most of the night in the bathroom.

CHAPTER 9

TRIALS AND TRIBULATIONS

We concentrated our emotions and energies into finding ways to improve Matthew's quality of life. But I would be lying if I said it was always easy.

Philip and Elisabeth's son Mark is four months younger than Matthew and he of course was developing "normally". Philip told us on one visit that they frequently did Matthew's exercises with Mark who thought they were a "hoot". I know Philip didn't mean to be insensitive but each time we saw them it highlighted the difference in physical development between the two boys. The gap was widening all the time. We had our gorgeous and intelligent little boy trapped in a body that worked against him, and Mark of course was gaining new skills all the time. Not usually given to self-pity or negativity some of these occasions were very poignant and difficult to smile through.

As I have repeatedly said our family and friends were wonderful: Their care and support was demonstrated in countless ways. Both sets of parents were very willing babysitters, chauffeurs and toy inventors. We remember both Dads, Harold and George, getting together to design a trolley for Matthew to push. He wasn't able to stand up unaided so they came up with a ladder type handle which he could use to pull himself up. It needed weights so as not to run away with him, but not be so heavy that he couldn't move it. Harold built it and Matthew loved it. He still needed someone behind him as his grip wasn't too clever and he was prone to an involuntary movement causing him to fall backwards, but the immense pride and pleasure he got from pushing this toy around was priceless.

Matthew loved feeling the ground beneath his feet, but getting his heels down and his feet flat was a problem because of the involuntary movements. Normal shoes couldn't cope with these constricting spasms. Jean Ward recommended Matthew should be measured for some "Piedro" boots. These boots are tailor made for each child. They are adapted to meet each specific need, so obviously correct measuring is essential, this meant another 3 monthly appointment on the calendar at the Orthotics department, but the boots were worth waiting for and helped enormously.

Jean was also keen for Matthew to have a "corner chair". This is a chair especially designed to prevent a child from arching backwards. The chair was sort of triangular shape, so the shoulders were very supported by high sides and back. It had a pommel in the front to separate the legs and so stretch the hips. A removable tray meant it was practical as well as comfortable. She lent us one for a while but they were in very short supply. So Uncle Colin being very clever made Matthew his own!

Pauline, Barry's sister; her husband Colin and Tim and Sarah loved spending time with Matthew. He often stayed the night with them and Tim and Sarah used to sit him up, surround him with cushions and count how many seconds he could stay up. This was one of his regular exercises but a lot more fun when being cheered on by your big cousins. Alan and Ann looked after Matthew when Barry and I had a weekend in Paris. They were also regular swimming volunteers on a Friday. Matthew loved spending time with their girls. Alan and Tim took their roles as Matthew's godfathers very seriously and have been a tremendous source of encouragement and support.

We had been working hard, teaching Matthew to roll over from his back to his front and vice versa. Matthew lay on the floor on his back (this was the easier way) and I knelt down beside him. One of his arms was extended above his head and then I gently pulled the opposite shoulder and hip towards me. For months and months this was a regular exercise, until one Friday evening when Matthew was about eighteen months old and he was lying on the floor on his back and then just rolled over! Barry was out working so I rang everybody to tell them, I was so excited, and so was Matthew!

From that moment on it became his way of moving independently. He could get from one side of a room to the other in no time! Determination and hard work had paid off again! Commando crawling was then just a small move away, at which point everywhere in the house became accessible! I could no longer take advantage of his good nature and feel confident he wasn't going to move from a given spot!

CHAPTER 10

NEW EXPERIENCES

At every opportunity we were keen for Matthew to try new things and develop his social skills.

An old friend from BT days invited us to bring Matthew along to the stables where she worked and kept her own horses. Linda introduced Matthew to an elderly pony called Julius; it was love at first sight! Many a happy Sunday afternoon found us walking up and down the lane behind Linda leading Matthew on his faithful steed. Not only was it a pleasure but it helped with his balance, strengthened his back and stretched his hips, so in terms of exercise it was very beneficial too.

Jean Ward told us about a swimming group for mums and babies held at a local special school every Thursday afternoon.

We went along and here I met other mums with children who had a wide range of special needs. It was so good to meet and swap experiences with kindred spirits. Having a disabled child is a very lonely experience even if you are surrounded by a loving family. So to be able to talk to other people sharing your experiences and difficulties was wonderful. But it wasn't all doom and gloom, we had lots of laughs too. Having a sense of humour and being able to see the funny side of things is necessary whatever life sends your way.

As a result of meeting these other mums, an idea was put into place that would reap benefits for us at a much later date. One of the mums was fund raising for a very special chair for her equally very special little girl. The chair was in essence an electric wheelchair but it had the capability to do other things. For instance at the touch of a button the seat could rise and also support the child in a standing position, opening up all sorts of opportunities for mischief! And of course independence!!

As you can imagine the price tag was just as impressive and fundraising efforts very challenging. From memory I think the Army became involved, Colchester being a major military garrison town, and with their enthusiasm on board the little girl finally became the proud owner of this super charger!

At the end of the day there were some funds over and the family rang me and asked if they could donate some of this money to us so that we could start fundraising for a similar chair for Matthew. This was obviously a very kind and generous offer but it gave us a huge dilemma.

By this time Matthew had started school at Thomas Wolsey and was working so hard at his physiotherapy,and his motivation to walk was so strong would having a chair take all that away? After a great deal of thought and soul searching we decided to decline their offer. We were able however to put them in touch with another family who had a little lad with Muscular Dystrophy and a chair would make a world of difference to him but more about that later.

When Matthew was three years old we were introduced to a Peripatetic teacher called Sue Fryman. Sue came to visit Matthew at home on alternate Friday afternoons. The boot of her car was crammed with toys of all descriptions. As you can imagine Sue's visits were eagerly awaited by Matthew and me! Sue's lovely calm and fun approach encouraged Matthew to explore a huge variety of toys which helped develop his play skills.

For once here was someone who wasn't just concerned to see how impossible it was for him to thread cotton reels! I'm sure many of you with a child with CP or any physical disability will have experienced that one!

As a reward Matthew's favourite toy from each session was left with him until her next visit. Matthew loved giant wooden floor puzzles so Sue had one specially made for him. It depicted the "Playschool" house and characters from one of his favourite TV programmes. Sue is a very special and talented lady extremely popular in our household

Dr Banyard, the school doctor, visited to assess Matthew and she thought he would benefit enormously from going to a local playgroup. I first tried the village group but it was not a good experience. Judging them is unfair because not everybody saw Matthew as we did, but suffice it to say there were more reasons presented to me as to why he shouldn't go than positive ones. The main ones being a question of Matthew's safety and what would happen in the event of a fire.

We found a playgroup in Wivenhoe, the next village up the road from Alresford who were keen to have Matthew join them. He had a welfare assistant Diane to help him integrate with all the activities. This was my first experience of leaving Matthew with strangers. The other children were totally accepting of Matthew and very soon he was making friends; me too! His social life extended to being invited to birthday parties and playing at other people's houses. Very often we travelled to and from playschool by train, which made it even more of an adventure.

Almost without exception everywhere we went and everyone we met was captured by Matthew's lovely sunny nature and sheer joie de vivre. I know I am biased but his smile could melt ice caps!!

Life, particularly mine, was packed with hospital visits, swimming, horse riding, exercises, speech therapy and playschool. From experience we knew this demanding schedule can effect even the strongest of relationships and ours was no exception. Barry and I decided we would have one evening a week to call our own. Our very good friends Lynne and Tony also led a very hectic life, and so we chose to spend every Wednesday evening together in a child free zone.

Sometimes we played badminton, but mostly spent the evening in our local. It is a tradition we still keep up today except that we have swapped Wednesday for Thursday and the pub for a cosy sofa and good natter. A young couple Liz and Brian babysat for us each week and they became great friends and supporters of Matthew. Liz's father was a local farmer and sometimes on a Saturday she would pick Matthew up and they spent a day on the farm, tractor rides and feeding the chickens were his favourite. The whole of Liz's family made Matt so welcome that they have remained friends with us all to this day!

In 1984 Alan ran in the London Marathon and raised a lot of money for the Spastics Society. In recognition of his achievement the local branch of the Spastics Society invited him to be a guest at the annual Christmas party. The party was held in a local nightclub and Matthew was asked to present a bouquet of flowers to the guest of honour, Helen Shapiro, who is a tremendous supporter of the society. Alan, Cheryl, Lynne and Tony came along too. Helen and Lynne got chatting and discovered they had played netball against each other during their schooldays.

Matthew strutted his stuff on the dance floor until the wee small hours: maybe that's when his love of night clubbing was born!!!

ANOTHER LITTLE ANECDOTE

My parents wanted to take Matthew to see Father Christmas. They took a very excited Matthew into Colchester one evening and into the Co-op which had the best Santa. Part of the toy department was converted into Santa's grotto and apparently Matthew's face was a picture as mum and dad pushed him through. That was nothing to the expression on his face when Father Christmas greeted them with "Hello George how are you?" Matthew was gobsmacked. Father Christmas and granddad were mates!! Life couldn't be more wonderful than that.

Incidentally, Father Christmas was a lovely man called Stan who had worked with dad years before but please don't tell Matthew.

Christmas has always been a great time in our family. My dad used to describe it as "A glorified Sunday with nuts!" But woe betide anyone who didn't enter wholeheartedly into the spirit of the celebrations! Matthew loves it too and one of his favourite things, like most children, was decorating the Christmas tree.

Challenging times! Putting the string of the decoration into his hand was the first hurdle, next holding him up to the tree, and then whoops! An involuntary movement sent the decoration flying and also several that had already made it onto the tree! But as always we persevered until the job was done. It's amazing but some of our decorations are as old as we are.

CHAPTER 11

A TALE OF TWO BUNNIES

To retell our story I am trying as far as I am able to keep events in chronological order. Some memories however are evoked by individual triggers and not synchronization, and so I have decided to punctuate the story with random and out of sequence tales, a couple of which I have already told you.

The following is a tale of two rabbits, more fondly remembered as "Bunnies".

Nanny and granddad were off to a village fete one Saturday afternoon and offered to take Matthew who was then about two years old. As we were decorating, this was a very popular offer. It transpires that at this fete there was a very large soft toy stall laden with mostly beautiful handmade animals. Nanny and granddad told Matthew to choose one and they would treat him.

Matthew looked long and hard and spotted a dark green tartan rabbit. To say it could have won first prize in any "Ugly parade" is an understatement. Its stuffing was uneven, its eyes didn't match, one ear stood up whilst the other collapsed and all was sewn together with very irregular stitches that allowed stuffing to spill whenever it was moved. (If the creator recognizes their handiwork please don't be offended but do read on!)

My parents tried very hard to persuade Matthew towards a cute and well made toy but he was emphatic "Bunny" was THE one.

Matthew loved him to bits and Bunny is probably one of the world's most travelled toys. He has been photographed in such diverse places as Niagra Falls, USA, Europe and most of the Cornish coast.

We have never understood what Matthew sees as he looks at Bunny for it isn't what most people see.

46

Bunny has been re stuffed and re stitched so many times and now resides in a plastic bag in our loft because the moths love him too.

The second rabbit arrived when Matthew was four years old. As I have previously mentioned we had a very large garden and as Matthew loved animals we thought it would be very nice for him to have a pet rabbit, and so the rabbit wouldn't be lonely maybe a guinea pig for company too.

Off we went to the garden centre to choose our new pets. The guinea pig was easy as they only had the one, a little white fluffy animal. Rabbits there were in abundance of every colour and type but only one that was brown and white. This was the one Matthew wanted and so we sought an assistant. She immediately looked concerned and said she would fetch the manager. A little puzzled by her reaction we waited for the manager to arrive. He took us to one side and suggested Matthew choose again. Matthew however was insistent this was the rabbit he wanted. (Yes I know this sounds familiar!) Okay so the story was that as a kitten our would be pet had fallen out of the nest and when its mother hauled it back she had bitten off one of its feet! (We have heard every rabbit's foot joke going) Matthew as we know could not be dissuaded so we took both animals home.

We bought a large hutch and Barry built them a lovely run. Ensconced in their new home they settled down together beautifully. Our vet checked over the rabbit and, although bemused by the story of the missing foot, declared him a very fit little specimen. Mathew named the guinea pig Ollie and the rabbit Dizzy. He spent many happy hours kneeling by their run watching their antics and poking dandelion leaves through the mesh. Both animals became very tame and enjoyed being handled.

Dizzy often came indoors and was quite happy to sit on Matthew's lap in the big armchair. I can't remember how it occurred but Dizzy developed a passion for Smarties and would follow a trail of them around the kitchen floor. Dizzy and Ollie lived to ripe old ages in rabbit and guinea pig years. They were the first of many such pets.

CHAPTER 12

LOSING HAROLD

Barry's career with the Prudential was progressing well. He had however turned down several opportunities for promotion. Promotion meant moving away from Colchester and we felt unable to leave the Colchester area because everything Matthew needed was right here, and the support we received from our family and friends was paramount.

Very sadly and suddenly, in April 1984 we lost one of our greatest supports, Barry's dad, Harold.

I have described on previous pages all the roles he fulfilled. Not only was he a great dad and grandfather, his talents for making and mending things were legendary. We used to tease him about having shares in araldite and WD40! There didn't seem to be a single thing he couldn't fix! When Barry was a young footballer Harold would be at every home game cheering him on, and then in later years they played many a round of golf together.

Harold and Matthew were great pals. Many hours Matthew spent on granddad's lap whilst he read from a large Richard Scarry book. The book contained pages of pictures of everyday items each with their name written underneath. Harold patiently read the words to Matthew, who would try to copy them, howls of laughter when he couldn't get it right and granddad repeating them over again. I think sometimes Matthew got them wrong on purpose just to make granddad laugh and play for extra time.

Harold was also a "magician" and performed magic tricks for all his grandchildren; their favourite was probably the red spider. The spider had a magnet underneath so if you got a second magnet and a tray you could make the spider move all by itself.

On family days out he and my dad would have competitions to see who could make the tea fastest on their little spirit stoves! Harold was a huge loss and we all miss him still.

FAMILY HOLIDAYS

For as long as I can remember there has always been a dog in my life. At this particular point in time our family dog was a yellow labrador called Bess. She was a retired Guide dog and threw herself enthusiastically into retirement to become a lovely, gentle and fun member of our pack. Matthew and Bess adored each other. Bess showed endless patience with him and, so what if an involuntary movement caught her across the snout. Being an impromptu pillow or ramp for his cars was fine by Bess.

Weather permitting most Saturday or Sunday afternoons Alan, Ann and the girls came over for a walk. Matthew now wearing Piedro boots was desperate to get out of his buggy and feel the ground beneath his feet. Supported either side by willing hands he practised walking. Aching backs gave in long before Matthew did.

It was often suggested to us that we should try to get some compensation for what had happened to Matthew surrounding his birth. Our reply in those days was always the same. No amount of money could erase Matthew's disabilities, and we were in a position to provide for all his needs. Barry was earning very well which enabled us to enjoy a comfortable lifestyle with lots of outings and wonderful holidays.

One such holiday we spent in Porth, Cornwall. The beach is gorgeous, you can drive right onto it and it has perfect sandcastle sand. Matthew couldn't run around on the beach like the other children but he could crawl, although he often head-butted the sand and ended up with a mouthful!

To find ways of entertaining him Barry became an absolute master at building not only sandcastles, but racing cars, boats, and planes. The landlord of our Guest House and fellow guests really entered into the spirit of Barry's sand creations and provided materials to make them even more fantastic. I remember one racing car having huge "exhausts" made with drainpipes, and a boat with real wooden seats. The resident ice cream van seller turned a very benevolent blind eye to the massive craters Barry made on the beach, around which he had to negotiate his van. Matthew and his marvellous sand machines were the envy of many other holiday making children and he often had company inside a cockpit or passenger seat!

Wendy with Matthew 9 days after his arrival in the world

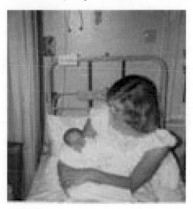

Mickey Mouse; one of the characters Barry had painted on Matthew's nursery wall

Granddad Harold and Matthew having great fun!!

Wendy and Matthew with Auntie Jean, Uncle Peter, cousins Alvin and Helen on a family trip to Scarborough in 1984

1960's Pop-star Helen Shapiro receives a bouquet from Matt at a charity night in 1986.

Barry, Matthew and Uncle Alan after Matt's triumphant ride in 1984!

Matthew riding a pony called 'Julius' with Auntie Pauline and Linda by his side.

Matt on his Pashley Pickle tricycle at Uncle Alan and Auntie Ann's in 1984

CHAPTER 13

THOMAS WOLSEY

Our next major consideration was Matthew's education. We visited our local village school but at that time because of all the extra curricular needs Matthew had it was not appropriate.

The only school in Essex catering especially for physically disabled children was the Southview School which was then in Braintree about 20 miles away, and actually part of an orthopaedic hospital. Jackie Stubbs worked at this school so she was keen for Matthew to go there. Southview School was very small: there were probably about 30 pupils on the register aged between 4 and 16.

Barry, Matthew and I went on a visit and we were impressed with what we saw. It was a very caring environment. All the staff there were talented and dedicated. The children appeared very happy, but we both felt it was not the right place for Matthew. Matthew needed to be stretched both physically and mentally. He has always thrived on competition and challenge. Southview was so small we didn't feel it could meet those needs. He would certainly have been the most physically able of the pupils there and as we know all kids need competition to motivate them.

Then there was the Thomas Wolsey School, also about twenty miles away but in Ipswich in the county of Suffolk.

We arranged a visit to the Thomas Wolsey and knew immediately this was the school for our son.

The Headmaster showed us round. Our first stop the Reception class with teacher Roz Rooney where Matthew was quite happy to stay whilst Barry and I continued our tour. There were over a hundred pupils with wide ranging physical difficulties. Some of the pupils were there just on a temporary basis as they recovered from accidents or surgery.

The facilities were very impressive, hydrotherapy pool, physiotherapy department, speech and occupational therapists plus a very successful school band.

Everything Matthew needed could be carried out by amazing staff and all under the one roof so to speak. As luck would have it there was a vacancy! Now all we had to do was convince the Local Education Authority. They immediately said "no". Funding was of course the big issue.

Their argument was that the Thomas Wolsey School was out of county so the transport costs would be greater and there was, as far as they were concerned, an appropriate school in Essex. I argued that, although the school was out of county the distance was the same as that of the Southview School so the transport costs would be the same.

They were already funding at least three other children from the Colchester area to go to Thomas Wolsey School so we weren't setting a precedent. In addition to this, I pointed out that money could be saved by Matthew having all his needs catered for in the one place. Not all of the therapies available at Thomas Wolsey School were on offer at the Southview School.

My main argument though was about Matthew himself, we felt Thomas Wolsey was the right place for our child. We were no different to any other parent wanting the best possible opportunities available, and as tax payers we couldn't agree to their mutterings about funding.

I had to make such a nuisance of myself bombarding the LEA with letters and phone calls.

Eventually in frustration and eventually in desperation, I wrote to our MP Sir Anthony Buck. This proved to be a very smart move because once we had his support the LEA finally capitulated and agreed to Matthew starting at Thomas Wolsey in September!

Matthew would travel to and from school by taxi, and his driver Dave Rothwell paid us a visit to introduce himself. Dave told us he would pick Matthew up at 8.00am each morning.

There were two other children in the taxi, a little lad from Frinton and a little girl from Colchester. Dave's mum rode in the back as escort.

It all sounded very exciting to Matthew, who was really looking forward to starting school, but, as most mums can identify, Matthew's first day at school was a really tough one for me.

I was lost and so anxious. He seemed such a little boy to be going so far away and having to cope alone in a strange environment, a situation I had fought so hard to put him in! I managed not to ring the school to find out how he was doing, they had promised to ring me if necessary.

He arrived home just after 4pm, exhausted but very happy to be going back the next day. Thoughtfully each child had a home/school diary to enable communication between the two.

Matthew soon made friends, in particular with a boy in his class from Colchester whose name was Hadj, and they would become best mates for years. I met Hadj's mum Shirley and we immediately clicked too.

During the school holidays we spent a lot of time together, either taking the boys swimming or to the cinema. Sometimes we just visited each other's homes. I remember "Transformers" being the "in" thing and we sat through every film as the boys loved them.

Both boys loved the TV series "He Man" and between them collected all the characters. They spent hours making up their own adventures.

Matthew and Hadj went on a Red Cross holiday one year and according to the Red Cross volunteers the boys were inseparable and true partners in crime, keeping all the volunteers on their toes but in fits of laughter at their antics! One day they planned to have a Porsche each, one in blue the other in red!

Once Matthew started school our lives, particularly mine, changed dramatically. As he was having all the therapy needed whilst in school we only saw Jean Ward during the school holidays. Sadly we said goodbye to Jackie, Sue and Thursday afternoon swims, a chapter of life much valued but now closed. Swimming was wonderful physiotherapy so losing our Thursday swim was a blow. Jean Ward however found out about a family session held in the same pool but on a Wednesday evening. As I have said Barry worked in the evenings and at this point I did not have my own car.

In came the ever supportive Uncle Alan. Every Wednesday evening he came straight from work in Ipswich picked us up and drove us into Colchester for the swim. The session was very popular, most of the children had disabilities such as Cystic Fibrosis, Down's Syndrome and CP, but it was great to see them enjoying the water with their siblings. Initially Alan's only interest was Matthew, but as the weeks went by and we got to know the other children and their families it became like a little club and we made many friends. The swimming teacher in charge, Wyn Robinson, gave expert tuition and with Alan's encouragement in the water Matthew became a competent swimmer. After each session Alan drove us home again: it was a weekly commitment he kept up for many years.

I have to refer back now to the Thursday afternoon swims and the offer made to us regarding funding for a special chair for Matthew. As I said we had declined the offer, but we met as a result of our new Wednesday swimming slot a very deserving candidate. His name was Trevor and he suffered from Muscular Dystrophy, an electric chair would change his life. Trevor was at the same school as Vicky, Alan's youngest daughter. He was a great little chap but his mobility was becoming severely impaired by this awful condition. I put the two families in touch and fundraising for his chair got a real kickstart. The chair made a huge difference to Trevor, we would sometimes see him at Alan and Ann's, or out and about in their neighbourhood with all the other children, just being one of the gang. It was great to witness.

Trevor's mum, Monica, phoned me some time afterwards to say they had some money over from their fundraising, and they would like to help Matthew in some way, was there anything he needed? A chair was still not the right thing for Matthew at this time, but we had been looking into getting him a computer. Because of his poor hand control a regular keyboard was not suitable, so we spoke to the IT specialist at Thomas Wolsey. He suggested a BBC computer with a specially adapted and expanded keyboard.

The keyboard was much larger and heavier than a regular one, the keys were set further apart and the letters were in "holes". A delay mechanism could be adjusted to allow Matthew more time to hit the right key, and courtesy of the extra weight it didn't fly off the table when Matthew had an involuntary movement. It was absolutely perfect, but again the cost was prohibitive.

Monica said go ahead and order it and we will pay for it. Monica got the local press involved, as obviously she wanted to keep people informed as to how their generous donations had been spent.

Once Matthew had the computer the local paper came and took our picture and they also wrote a lovely article titled "Smiles that say thanks a lot!"

The computer was invaluable not only for Matthew to work with, he also discovered "Space Invaders" although very often he had to fight Barry for a turn!

Very sadly Trevor lost his fight against this terrible disease some years later but his legacy and memories of him live on.

Back to Thomas Wolsey, Barry and I swung our efforts whole-heartedly into supporting the school in any way we could. Barry was voted onto the committee of the "Friends" and I did as much voluntary work as I could.

The Friends worked tirelessly to raise funds for the school, with their main ambition to build an indoor swimming pool. I wrote to every organisation imaginable asking for their help or donations towards the swimming pool fund. Cheryl, bless her, typed every letter for me. What quickly became apparent was that the School needed charitable status before any donations would be forthcoming. So this was what we arranged as soon as possible!

All the school events were a must in our social calendar. At the annual summer fete Barry used his minor celebrity status and invited folk to part with their money and take him on at "Beat the goalie".

One year Barry was unable to come to the summer fete, but Matt and I went. Matthew wanted to enter the Fancy Dress competition as a Punk. I made him a black suit; he had safety pins everywhere and the pièce de resistance was bright pink and spiky hair!

Barry was a bit taken aback when we came home and he saw for the first time Matthew's new hairdo, especially as we were going out on a boat trip that evening with some work colleagues and so obviously we had to look our best! I reassured Barry the hair dye would wash out immediately just as it said on the can but as you have probably guessed it didn't!

Matthew turned quite a few heads that night not for being disabled but because of his bright pink hair!

The Bonfire night and Christmas parties were not only great fun but raised lots of money for the school funds too. Every event was well supported making all the hard work put in by the volunteers worthwhile.

One of the "friends" of the school was a publican who kept a beautiful old pub in Thornham Magna. Every summer he hosted a three mile Fun Run. The pub was open all day and the school band played. This event was particularly popular and always got tremendous support.

Barry and Alan had taken up running and were very keen half marathon runners. Matthew, although unable to run, was desperate to take part, especially as he had recently been lent a Pashley Pickle tricycle by the Health Authority.

The "Pickle" was a specially adapted tricycle, fitted with stirrups on the pedals to keep his feet in place, and a seat complete with bar and belt to secure his trunk.

He was lethal on it!! No need for any fitness training when Matthew was riding his trike, just lots of speed and stamina to keep up with him because he never could work the brakes. As you have probably guessed Matthew was going to do the Fun run on his bike with Barry and Alan running alongside him. Well that was the plan! I remember being at the Finish line with my mum and dad all ready to cheer Matthew on and encourage him to complete the run, after all 3 miles is a long way for a little fellow!

Suddenly in the distance coming round the final bend on two wheels was a little blonde head wearing the biggest grin you ever did see, running closely behind a very proud dad and uncle. Not only had he completed the race he was the first one home! We eventually managed to catch him and bring him to a stop. We grown-ups were always the best form of brakes!

Competitiveness was encouraged at Thomas Wolsey and competitive Matthew surely was, especially with his friends! During his time at Thomas Wolsey he took part in the Stoke Mandeville games. This was a competition organized for children from Special schools around the country a kind of mini para-olympics. Matthew was competing in various events including Bocchia (a version of indoor bowls), swimming and walking. He maintains to this day he was robbed of the Bocchia title! And although he refused to swim, complaining the water was too cold, he did have some success in the walking races.

Another great friend of Matthew's was Damien. There was huge rivalry between the two, especially when it came to walking or swimming. If, for example, Matthew had physiotherapy first and had managed to walk five steps then Damien would aim for six. When Damien swam one width of the pool Matthew had to do two, so you get the picture, and I am sure if you were to ask Matt or Damien they would say that this competitiveness played a vital part in both their developments.

Incidentally, Damien was the little lad in hospital that Jean had helped with his Bliss board all those years before!

The swimming pool became a reality and was a great asset to the pupils and their families.

Another new addition to the school was Carol McCarthy. Joining the staff as a new teacher she was an immediate hit. Young, bubbly, very enthusiastic and funny, the kids adored her.

Carol wanted to stage a Christmas musical that would involve every child in the school. This was such an ambitious project as most of the kids were either wheelchair bound or used some form of walking aid.

Matthew's mo was now a rollator. It was an ambitious task, but with Carol's determination, a very elaborate Nativity story, and unshakeable belief in the kids, "Stargazers" was born and proved a tremendous success. Every child performed with pride, confidence and enthusiasm, earning themselves total respect from the audience and each other. There was not a dry eye at the end of each performance, and I still can't watch the video without a tear. Matthew played the innkeeper.

Hadj left Thomas Wolsey and went into mainstream education. Like Matthew he is a very bright chap in spite of his physical difficulties. Hadj went on to win The Great North Run Wheelchair Race twice; in 1998 and 1999.

We had discovered that if Matthew was making progress with his speech then physically he came to a plateau and vice-versa and talking with other mums I found this to be common. Motivation to do both is then very challenging. Losing Hadj as a classmate left Matthew with fewer children able to speak with him. Very aware of this Mrs Rooney came up with a cunning plan. Mrs Rooney's husband taught at a local primary school in Ipswich, close to Thomas Wolsey. She suggested Matthew go on a visit and maybe spend every Friday afternoon with them in a mainstream class.

We agreed Matthew could benefit from spending time there. This arrangement hadn't been tried before so Matthew was a bit of a guinea pig. It proved to be a very successful experiment and got us thinking that maybe we could try and make the same arrangement at our local primary school in Alresford. Loneliness was a problem just rearing its inevitable head. Very often the school holidays in Essex and Suffolk did not coincide, so Matthew was yet to have an opportunity to meet any local children. Our friend's children all went to school in Essex so for some school holidays Matthew had no one to play with.

The following paragraphs are Matthew's own thoughts and memories of his time at Thomas Wolsey.

MATTHEW'S MEMORIES OF THOMAS WOLSEY SCHOOL

Although memories of actually starting at Thomas Wolsey School elude me, I possess some fond memories of my time there.

One of my fondest memories included the fetes, which took place during the summer. Although I would never tell my dad to his face, I have to concede that I was very proud that my dad, "The Legend", was the goalie in "beat the goalie" competitions which he did each year.

The fetes were the epitome of great family days out and the one that stands out the most was the one where everyone had to dress up, and I can attribute the beginning of my hair loss to this occasion. My mum dressed me up as a punk-rocker and even dyed my hair pink! See Mum, you started my fascination with dying my hair!

My time at Thomas Wolsey was a happy one for me as I made some fantastic friends such as Damien Gentleman, Jamie Carver and Kevin Sadler. Kevin sadly passed away far too young.

Despite having fantastic teachers, my time at the school wasn't really about learning subjects, but more about developing myself physically i.e. walking and talking. I found physiotherapy a right chore and a lot of the time felt like giving up (although this was never really an option for me with my family!). So, physio, did it work? I can safely say at the tender age of 30 that physio definitely worked, but it was greatly assisted by having competition in the form of Damien who acted as my physio partner.

Although it pains me greatly to admit it, I can be very stubborn and overly competitive, as was Damien, so our competitiveness proved to be one of our prized assets. If I walked five steps, Damien would walk six and so on, to the point where we'd just collapse on each other and wait for the next day or activity to commence our rivalry once more!

It wasn't just physio in which Damien and I competed, oh no! If anything could be made into a contest, we did it!

Bocchia brought out both mine and Damien's competitive streaks and I think Damien will admit I had the upper hand more often than not. Both Damien and I participated in the Stoke Mandeville Games along with others to compete in sports against other special schools. I must admit Damien, who went on to become world champion at Bocchia later on in life, did in fact win the Bocchia tournament on this occasion. However, I have always maintained I was the victim of a sexist judge and was ousted in the 1st round by a girl, despite me clearly winning two games in a best of three! Ashamedly, I wimped out of the swimming contest due to the water looking to be too cold, oops! I did however regain some pride by winning the 100m rollator race despite having a fall. My bunny, which I'm sure mum has previously mentioned, was with me every step of those hundred metres, for he sat in my satchel which was attached to my rollator!

My memories of Thomas Wolsey are far too numerous for me to capture here but without a doubt I would not be the person I am now without them and I would like to thank those who were part of my life then and hope I have made them proud of the life I'm living, especially my dear friend Kevin, who was a huge inspiration to all with his unwavering happiness.

BARRY

Going back to when Matt was attending Thomas Wolsey School I inadvertently could have killed him!!

He came home from school in the taxi on this particular day and he can't have been much more than five years old. It was raining very hard and Wendy and I decided that we would have Spaghetti Bolognese for dinner that night. I had realized that we had no mushrooms in the fridge so dashed out onto the front lawn where loads were growing! I picked enough and brought them in. The resulting meal nearly killed Wendy and me (there was obviously at least one toadstool in amongst the mushrooms). It wasn't obvious to me when I picked them! Anyway fortunately Matt didn't want Spag Bol. How really fortunate was that? It was probably the worst and most ill Wendy and I have felt in all our lives so far.

On the plus side I have also saved his life, but more of that later.

CHAPTER 14

SANDOWN

Before I go on with Matt's education plans I would like to include another little anecdote.

In the summer after Matt started at Thomas Wolsey we went on a holiday to the Isle of Wight with Alan, Ann and all their girls. Our accommodation was two adjoining flats in the lovely resort of Sandown. The weather was glorious, very hot and sunny. We had a marvellous time exploring the island and enjoying lots of time on the beach and of course everybody's favourite, Blackgang Chine.

One particularly hot afternoon we decided some time off the beach would be good for us all and a game of Crazy golf was the most popular idea. As Sandown Zoo was right next door to the crazy golf Matt and I would spend the afternoon there. I was happily pushing Matt around the zoo and enjoying watching all the animals. We then came to what looked like a dark tunnel: it was the Reptile house. Unfortunately I have a phobia of snakes and wasn't keen to go in but Matt of course insisted that we do!

The zoo was very quiet that day and there was nobody else around as we entered the tunnel. Once inside we heard a voice calling "Help me please". As we got nearer we saw a solitary lady with a huge Boa constrictor wrapped around her! She said "Please get this thing off me, the keeper has gone to fetch a camera to take my picture and said he would be back in a few seconds, but I'm now terrified because I can't see its head!" Yes, and so was I! I told the poor lady I couldn't touch the snake even if my life depended on it but we would stay with her until the keeper returned, giving her a running commentary on where the snake's head was. Matt thought it was hilarious!

True to his word the keeper did return very shortly and took the lady's photo. He was greatly amused by the whole episode and then very kindly gave us a guided tour of the house and a description of each snakes endearing qualities! In spite of which I still fail to appreciate their charms! After our tour the lady bought Matt a very large ice-cream as a reward for his gallantry. He couldn't wait to meet up with the rest of the gang and tell them about our adventures.

CHAPTER 15

BACK TO THE EDUCATION PLAN.

Mrs Rooney's idea of Matt spending time going to "normal" school in Ipswich had worked really well and so we started to explore the possibility of Matthew, now seven years old, attending our local mainstream primary school.

Our first job was to approach the Headmaster and see how he felt about it. Integration at that time was still a new concept.

The headmaster agreed in principle to give it a try, providing Matthew had full time welfare support. Thomas Wolsey was very keen as they felt academically Matthew had outgrown them and needed to spread his wings. They also promised that if it didn't work out Matthew was welcome back there at any time.

Once the two Headmasters agreed, we faced the inevitable battle of convincing the Local Education Authority. As you may recall I had all but sold my soul to the devil persuading the same Authority to let Matthew go to Thomas Wolsey!

Learning from past experiences we again enlisted the help of our local MP Sir Anthony Buck, who came into bat for us again. After a long campaign they eventually agreed to Matthew going to Alresford for two days a week, with funding for a welfare assistant. The first assistant was very keen to help in any way she could. She had two boys at the school and enlisted their help to break the ice as it wasn't all straightforward, Matthew was different. He couldn't walk without his rollator, he had impaired speech, constantly dribbled and had involuntary movements. It would be naïve to say everybody welcomed him.

We found folk were divided into three groups. Some just stared and avoided him, some totally ignored him and some just accepted the whole package. Luckily the third group was in the majority. He made friends very quickly and once people got to know him and me, a social life soon developed.

I remember one Sport's day his teacher approached me and said some of the children in his class didn't think it fair that Matthew couldn't take part. They had got together and thought it would be a good idea to have a walking and a cycling race that could include Matthew. We were, as you can imagine, absolutely overwhelmed.

His "Pickle" went into school with volunteers holding a crash mat on the finish line to help him stop, as he still hadn't learnt to use the brakes.

The walking race was something else, three or four of the children waited just short of the finish line so Matthew was not the last one to cross. We know only too well that children can be very cruel at times but they can also be equally kind and sensitive. Barry and I were not the only parents feeling very proud on that day.

BARRY RECALLS:

Matt's love of sport was now starting to develop. Alas! it obviously wasn't to be for Matt to follow my footballing path, but, much to our dismay, Matt showed a great deal of interest in football from an early age and even a desire to play!

We bought a small goal net and Matt would play in the garden in goal on his poor leather-like knees. Despite his disability it was apparent that he had actually got some ability and was soon diving around, effectively saving and blocking shots hit by his Dad who gave him no quarter whatsoever!

Matt also played cricket and his bowling was "something else" once he could release "the bloody ball". His words not ours! He used his right hand to bat with and hit the ball whilst on his "poor knees"! When playing cricket and batting Matt was perfectly normal in that when given out he would kick off and be a really bad loser. Again I would give him no quarter and generally Uncle Alan was quite firm with him as well.

Matt played football at primary school and generally was included by his peers. He actually played in two school matches for one half in each for Alresford County Primary. His participation in football lessened at secondary school though his interest in the game probably grew.

I have included some of Matt's memories of this change in his life.

MY TIME AT ALRESFORD PRIMARY SCHOOL:

First and foremost I have to thank my parents, Thomas Wolsey School and the staff at Alresford Primary School for making it happen after a typical battle with the education authorities.

Going to school is an ordeal for any child and it was no different for me. It was very daunting being the only disabled kid in the school. Although I do not have any distinct memories during this period I do remember the other children being kind, treating me like a novelty as they looked at me through curious eyes.

I did make friends with Adam and Ben Lowing, sons of my carer Jackie Lowing, and I enjoyed going to play at their home many times. My best friend throughout my days at Alresford School was Lucy Hammond. She treated me like any other child and was one of the two lovely daughters of Dawn Hammond who became another one of my carers. Lucy was and still is a lovely, caring and genuine young lady. It was Lucy who was responsible for adapting one of the events in our sport's day to include a bike race so that I could take part on my infamous Pashley Pickle tricycle. The finish line for me was a strategically placed crash mat due to me being unable to operate the brakes! Thanks Lucy.

Like Thomas Wolsey, I have far too many memories to include in Mum's book, but one that stands out greatly is when I made the school football team! Terry Smith, our sport's teacher, organized a football match against Brightlingsea School and I was picked to play goalkeeper for twenty minutes. Since being at Alresford I had developed a love for the "beautiful game" and attended football training

73

after school as well as playing at lunchtimes and attending P.E. sessions.

At this point in time it is important that I emphasize that I couldn't walk unaided so crawled on my knees, whether it was on a nice grassy pitch or a muddy bog, it didn't matter when a football was being kicked about. So, the match was played on a sunny winter's day and I am kneeling in the centre of a normal sized goal trying my best to emulate my dad by not conceding a goal on my debut! Brightlingsea got a corner and one of their players, Andrew Edgerton scored with a sweet kneeing volley which went in two feet over my head but sportingly he did not claim it.

Andrew later on became a good friend of mine when we met up again in secondary school. I do not remember the score from that game but a few months later we had a return match at Brightlingsea school and I was allowed to play in goal again. I remember it well because in the twenty minutes I played I made some good saves and only conceded one goal, but by the end of the game we lost 5-1. I can brag that I was better than my replacement – Dusty Bin! Being able to play a part in both matches meant a great deal to me and I thank Brightlingsea again for allowing it to happen.

CHAPTER 16

A PACKAGE FROM HEAVEN- AKA NIKKI

Barry and I had never intended Matthew to be an only child but despite five years of infertility treatment we had not been successful.

I won't dwell on this period too much but anybody unlucky enough to experience infertility will understand how heartbreaking it is and I extend my sincere sympathies and best wishes to you. Your lives become a circle of temperature taking, very invasive investigations, severe loss of dignity and extreme disappointment as each month rolls by.

Neither one of us was to "blame" but we each had problems, and after about four unsuccessful years it was suggested Barry have some investigations done at "Barts" hospital in London. The team at "Barts" recommended he have some minor surgery. He was understandably terrified, but agreed to the operation taking place after our holiday.

In the summer of 1986 we booked a two-week holiday in Cornwall. We made sure when we booked the holiday that our accommodation was on the ground floor. However when we arrived the hotel had changed hands, and the previous owner had not passed on our request. Our room was at the top of a very steep, narrow and winding staircase. I sat on the bed saying "This isn't what we ordered, this won't do at all." The new owners were extremely sorry but as they were fully booked there was nothing they could do. The manager even offered us his own bungalow!

After a few phone calls we found a lovely hotel overlooking Porth Bay. Our fellow guests were a great bunch and made a fuss of Matthew. His favourite song at the time was Stevie Wonder's "I just called to say I love you". He wouldn't go to bed until the band had played it and each night happily they obliged. The hotel's babysitting service meant we were able to enjoy some quality time to ourselves.

During the holiday I experienced some dizzy spells, so on our return I visited Dr Snell. He examined me and then sat back at his desk making notes. Typically he peered over the top of his spectacles and said he was delighted to inform me I was finally pregnant! The baby was due at the end of February. We were over the moon and Barry was off the hook!

My second pregnancy was as uncomplicated as the first until I had my three-month scan. Two days after which I got a phone call from the hospital telling me the baby's leg measurements were too small which could indicate Spina Bifida. They recommended I have a more detailed scan with a gynaecologist on the Monday morning. I immediately rang Dr Snell in total panic demanding his reassurance. Of course he couldn't give it, but in his usual honest and no nonsense way told me that should the scan show the baby was handicapped, I must consider a termination and then try again. In his opinion I should also insist on having Amniocentesis.

I suffered from recurring nightmares each night; they were always the same and included the words I had spoken when we had first arrived in Cornwall. In that unsuitable room I had said, "This isn't what we ordered, this won't do at all." But in my dream I was saying those words to a tiny, grotesque bundle, wrapped in a blanket and placed in my arms.

The weekend before my scan was the longest of our lives. As usual Pauline, Colin, Alan and Ann were there for us. They came over on the Saturday night for a Chinese meal and spent the evening having a laugh, trying to stay positive and blot out the unthinkable.

Early on Monday morning Barry and I arrived at the hospital and I had managed not to pass the two litres of water I was advised to drink before the scan.

When the scan was completed the consultant told us he was confident that the baby was fine and developing normally. Obviously he couldn't give a 100% guarantee but he was very optimistic. He advised against the amniocentesis because this can actually cause problems to the baby.

As you can imagine Barry and I were so relieved to hear his positive comments. We had discussed it long and hard and had already decided against a termination. No matter what the outcome this baby was desperately wanted.

Matthew discovered he was going to have a brother or sister whilst he was having a haircut. Hairdresser Win had cut his hair many times and was expert at rolling with the involuntary movements. We were chatting away as you do when she asked if we wanted any more children. At this precise moment Matthew's head was bent forward as she trimmed around the nape of his neck. Rather naively thinking that if Matthew couldn't see me he couldn't hear me I mouthed that I was four months pregnant. His head shot up and he was beaming.

Obviously that evening we had a long chat about it and Matthew put in his order for a little sister with long dark hair. She was to be called Nikki.

We explained it could be a brother but Matthew was having none of it, he was adamant it was going to be a girl. Dr Snell looked after me very well as he always had done and, after discussing birth options with him we decided on an elective caesarean.

January 1987 saw a very heavy snowfall, and depending on the skill of the snowplough operator, Alresford was intermittently cut off from civilisation and also the national grid! I was very worried in case the baby arrived early, but was quickly reassured by my husband that it wouldn't be a problem as a helicopter could land on the field behind us and airlift me to hospital! This had already happened to a lady in the next town so Barry had complete confidence in Plan B.

The snow cleared and we decided to change our central heating to gas and also have a new kitchen fitted. The work would obviously be finished before the baby arrived. How dumb were we!

Sunday January 25th I was restless all day. Barry had been busy decorating and at 9pm decided he had done enough to earn himself a bath and the nice big scotch he had promised himself. He did ask first if "Am I all right to have this, you're not going to give birth tonight are you?" He had just got the glass to his lips when I yelled "Stop, my waters have broken". Deja-vu!!!

Within a short time Pauline and Colin had brought Denise over to look after Matthew and we set off for the Maternity hospital.

Just like our first time we were excited but understandably full of trepidation. Once there I remember feeling sorry for the staff on duty. Barry was so assertive and determined that nothing should go wrong this time. He insisted I see a consultant immediately and it was decided I have my section early on Monday morning. The Anaesthetist announced Nikki's arrival by telling Barry all Matthew's wishes had come true!

Nikki weighed 4lbs, small but absolutely perfect. She was taken to SCBU where she met her big brother and grandma a few hours later. We all knew her entry into the world was very different from her brother's. Apart from a little jaundice she was fine.

Because they weren't very busy Nikki stayed in SCBU for a few days to allow us some time to get the heating and water supply sorted out at home as we were virtually living in one room. Matthew had the day off school to welcome her home. This little bundle was to grow up to be not only his little sister but also his best friend, chief protector, senior taskmaster, general "gopher" and his biggest but only one truly qualified critic!

Nikki was very like her brother as a baby, happy and contented. Shortly after she was born it was my mum and dad's Ruby wedding. We hosted a small party for them and Nikki was of course the star of the show. She was passed around for lots of cuddles, all under the ever watchful eyes of her big brother. Matthew made it his duty to remind everyone to support her head and that she preferred to be held upright.

Nikki was another victim of three-month colic, only it was much worse than Matthew's had been. She would cry and scream virtually nonstop for about six hours. It started as soon as Matthew came home from school and Barry was heading out the door to work. Nothing could pacify her for more than a few minutes. We tried everything, warm baths, rocking, gripe water, soft music, loud music, massage and pacing the floor. Then suddenly she fell asleep usually about 10.30pm, just before Barry came home from work commenting on how peaceful it all was!

For some reason the only person able to soothe her quickly was our friend Tony. On our regular Wednesday evenings Tony walked around the lounge with her over his shoulder and after a few minutes, as if by magic, she fell asleep. Unfortunately for us Lynne could not spare him every day!

The colic stopped, as it usually does, as suddenly as it started and we settled into our new routine.

Matthew was keen to help look after Nikki in any way he could, his favourite thing was to rock her in her bouncy chair, but because of his involuntary movements, sometimes she was almost catapulted into orbit and loved it. I firmly believe this was the beginning of her love for white knuckle rides! Matt takes up the story here!

Matt:

START OF THE BIG BRO DUTIES!

As corny as it seems, the day my little sis entered this world was by far the best day of my life and in a way the start of my life. It is true I was very, very, very lucky to have a family and friends such as mine, for which no word can explain my gratitude. However, looking back at life before Nikki, almost everything revolved around me and was constantly being grateful to everyone for helping me.

Now, writing this is extremely difficult as I try to get what I'm saying across correctly so bear with me. If I sound ungrateful then I've failed to write what I'm thinking. As I've just mentioned, before Nikki's arrival, everything pretty much revolved around me (every child's dream) but admittedly I was dealing with the fact I was disabled. I couldn't do much for myself, let alone for anyone else, so as much as I was and still am forever in my parents, family and friends debt I was a frustrated child because I could not repay their help and undying support and just hoped that by bettering myself I would go some way to show my gratitude.

Then the event that changed my entire life occurred, Nikki Jane Smith was born! To say I was excited during Mum's pregnancy is a huge understatement, so when grandma came to stay and Dad came into my bedroom late at night to tell me he was taking mummy to hospital to give birth, it felt like Christmas Eve times a million! Well, after dad came and told me, all chance of getting to sleep was non-existent and so I remember sitting at the dining table with Grandma eagerly awaiting the phone call, and then, after what seemed forever, it came! I had the greatest present I have ever been given – a sister! For which I can never thank Mum and Dad enough!

Well, normally when a sibling is born it is common for the first child to get green eyed when they now have to share people's affections, but not I! I was a very proud 'Big Bro' and loved showing her to people and learnt my biggest ever lesson. I had to be a big bro and therefore needed to be helpful. Now I was and never will be any good at changing nappies but, as Mum has mentioned, I could make Nik laugh by using the 'baby catapult' which I'm sure nowadays would be totally frowned upon. Nik used to suffer with colic and so would cry a lot. So when I got back from school I'd try the 'baby catapult', but if that didn't work, there was one thing that would fix an upset Nik, and that was nudging her stomach (gently) with my forehead. Many times she would be laughing her head off with my head on her belly. Nik was perfect and I loved her being a baby. However, she wouldn't talk to me! I must have asked Mum and Dad everyday "when will she talk? I can't wait." Boy she certainly makes up for it now! (Love you Nik).

I am aware this is Mum's book so will not harp on but just to help you appreciate how much Nikki's arrival changed my life, it was the first proper time that I realized I could do stuff for myself, and more importantly – others! It was a major thing for me and is an enormous reason for who I am today.

CHAPTER 17

BATTLES AND TRAGEDY

Liz and Brian, our regular babysitters, set a date for their wedding and Liz asked if I would make her bridesmaids' dresses for her. We had great fun going to choose materials etc. After they married, Liz's younger sister Shirley took over the Wednesday night babysitting service. Shirley was as popular with Matthew and Nikki as Liz had been.

It wasn't long after this that Shirley met a young man called Jim, a soldier stationed at Colchester. Jim was a very tall softly spoken King's Own Scottish Borderer. When Jim was not on duty he came with Shirley. Matthew thought Jim was great: they shared a love of military aircraft and spent hours together looking through books and magazines.

Because Barry worked every weekday evening Sunday was Matthew's favorite night of the week. Every Sunday evening as I was getting Nikki ready for bed Matthew and Barry started to prepare for a "battle". This was a work of art and an extreme lesson in patience.

Matthew had a large collection of metal toy soldiers and they had to be deployed strategically around the lounge. It was painstaking. Matthew always had a battle plan and knew exactly where each soldier had to be placed. The battle involved about 150-200 soldiers, each standing up, either behind wooden buildings or army vehicles. One can only imagine the frustration Matthew must have felt when one involuntary movement could knock down in a second what had taken ages to prepare. His patience was formidable.

Next came the really clever and fun part. Barry and Matthew each had a plastic spring loaded gun that fired ....ping pong balls!

Matthew knelt on the floor, gun and left hand wedged between his knees and thighs. With his right hand he pulled the trigger. He was unable to load the gun or pull the spring back but this Barry did for him with unfailing patience. It gave them both a great deal of pleasure which was sadly brought to a sudden end.

Shirley and Jim were married in Wivenhoe on a gorgeous hot summer's day. Jim looked very handsome in his uniform and Shirley made a beautiful bride. Matthew was very proud to have his photo taken with them.

Shortly after the wedding they were posted to Germany. Whenever they came home on leave they paid us a visit and on one of the visits Jim told us that he had been guarding Rudolph Hess in Spandau prison. It wasn't long before Shirley became pregnant and little Daniel was born in Germany.

Jim's next tour of duty was Northern Ireland. Shirley moved back to her parent's home in Wivenhoe and was a regular visitor with little Daniel. Nikki and Daniel enjoyed being together and shared a passion for Thomas the Tank Engine. Just before Christmas 1989 Jim had a short leave and they all came to see us. As Jim was leaving Barry told him "Keep your head down mate, see you in the New Year". Shirley and I made plans to see each other on the Wednesday morning to go into Colchester to do some Christmas shopping.

On the 9pm news on Tuesday evening the lead story was that two soldiers had been killed in Northern Ireland. I remember saying to Barry how worried Shirley must be when she heard news like that.

At six o' clock the next morning the phone rang. It was Liz in hysterics, Jim had been one of those two soldiers.

Jim had been killed by the IRA at a checkpoint in County Fermanagh. He was gunned down whilst trying to warn his colleagues of the suspicious approaching vehicle.

I do not have the words to describe how terrible the following days, weeks and months were. Jim's funeral took place in Wivenhoe and he was buried in the cemetery with full military honors. Anyone who has been to a service like this will testify as to how chilling the experience is, especially when those shots are fired over the grave.

It was so incredibly sad, a week before Christmas and a month before Daniel's first birthday. Shirley looked so tiny but was tremendously brave throughout the ceremony with her very close and supportive family by her side. A tragedy such as this is like a stone thrown into a pond, the ripples spread and change the surface but, unlike the surface of the pond, life never returns the same. Lives are touched and changed forever.

It is a very small thing in the grand scale of life, but Matthew and Barry never had the heart for another Sunday battle. Many years have now passed since Jim's untimely death, but remembering those dark days and of course the happy ones still brings a lump to my throat. It had a profound effect on Matt who continues:

Matt:

FAREWELL TO ARMS AND A DEAR FRIEND:

I don't think there are any words that can describe the way I and the rest of us felt about the loss of Jim. I was eight years old and Jim was one of my best mates and often spoke about how he hoped to be a dad one day. Well he was; only for a little while before he was cruelly taken away, but I know how much he loved Shirley and little Daniel so try and take some comfort that he experienced what many people do not. However, at the time I was so enraged and gutted that I wrote a poem for Jim and it helped me to come to terms with his great loss, but sadly I cannot remember the words.

As Mum mentioned, most Sunday evenings were spent doing battle with Dad, and before Jim's untimely passing, this was the highlight of the week, apart from continuing our rivalry whilst fishing. If Dad and I had been advisers to General Haig, World War One may have ended a lot sooner as both the deployment of our soldiers resulted in each other's frustration, especially having fifty shots at one soldier, who was propped against a wall and so would not fall over! It was special to spend time with Dad as he worked hard during the week, but after Jim passed away neither of us had the appetite for our battles anymore and called an Armistice. However, it wasn't long before Dad and I shared a new love – football!

CHAPTER 18

JERSEY

The first and only time I can recall Matthew showing any signs of resentment towards his little sister was at Stansted airport. We were off on holiday to Jersey, Grandma was with us and she was going to celebrate her 80th birthday whilst we were away.

Waiting in a departure lounge can be trying particularly when you have young children. Nikki was 18 months old, and, to keep her amused, she was pushing her empty buggy up and down the lounge with grandma walking behind her. Matthew sat beside me watching this little scene very carefully. I shall never forget the look on his face as he said, "How come Nikki can do that and I can't?" I don't truly remember exactly what my reply was, but it was something about life being very unfair at times and yes it was true he couldn't walk and run like Nikki but there were other things he could do very well. He was putting so much effort into walking and standing up so, if he tried very hard with his physio, maybe one day he would be able to chase Nikki about. Barry did not hear the conversation we were having and he took a photo of us. Every picture tells a story.

The holiday was great, gorgeous weather and lovely accommodation. It was Nikki's first real experience in a swimming pool, which she insisted on calling the "wet, wet". At every opportunity she wanted to be in the water, even waking us up at 5am one morning clad in Matthew's shorts and wearing her armbands! All ready for a dip!

Grandma's birthday was the 4th August and all the family sent bouquets of flowers. That night Barry, Matthew and I took Grandma out for a celebration dinner. Nikki was looked after by hotel staff. It was a very special evening.

On a visit to Paradise Gardens near St Helier we literally bumped into Roy Castle.

There was a photo shoot for the Battle of the Flowers parade going on and Roy was "Mr Battle" for that year. Matthew had always been a fan of the television programme Record Breakers which was presented by Roy Castle, so he was really excited when Roy came over to speak to him. Roy spent a long time chatting to us and posing for photos with Matthew, taking great care and patience that Matthew's shirt was pulled down and his chin dribble free. Over lunch he stopped by our table and drew a cartoon on Matthew's place mat, which I believe Matthew still has. He was a really lovely man whose death from cancer was a huge loss to everybody whose life he touched. We didn't tell anybody we had met him when we got home but just waited to see their faces when we showed our holiday slides!

Our favourite place in Jersey was Gorey Castle. We had great fun racing up and down the grassy slopes with Matthew and Nikki in their buggies. I was on a personal mission to find the location of the "Bureau des Étrangers" and also the car driven by John Nettles in the popular television series "Bergerac".

In hindsight it was also the first time Matthew became really aware of his physical limitations, the incident at the airport being the first realisation. One day on Greve de leq beach some children were playing in a rock pool when they noticed Matthew crawling along the beach towards them. One boy in particular started to poke fun at Matthew and call him names. Before Barry or I could do anything the small person walking at

Matthew's side raised a right hook that sent the boy backwards into a muddy puddle! Honour satisfied, the children all played happily together as if nothing had happened and Matthew's champion had revealed herself!

On the same day that we flew to Jersey our best friends Cheryl and Alan were also taking to the skies but not on holiday. Alan's career had taken the family to a new life in Cincinnati USA. Cheryl phoned one day and said "I have some good news and some bad news. The bad news is we are moving further away than we originally thought, but the good news is you are going to the States next year for your holidays!"

Cheryl and I are lifelong friends, our mums met when they were expecting our respective big sisters. She has always allowed me to bend her ear and get whatever grievance I had/have off my chest. Cheryl was the first person I turned to when whatever battle I was fighting with the education authorities got frustrating and tough.

Barry and Alan had been friends for years since way back when Scooters were the "In thing". Barry had a Lambretta whilst Alan was a Vespa man.

Matthew really enjoyed spending time with Andrew and Paul, Alan and Cheryl's sons, who were always patient and fun playmates. Barry is Andrew's godfather and I am godmother to their third son Christopher. Cheryl is Nikki's godmother. Christopher is a year and two days older than Nikki and at this point in time they didn't take much notice of each other but times change! As you can imagine, although we were genuinely thrilled about this wonderful opportunity that had come their way, we knew we would miss them dreadfully. They came over to say their goodbyes and Cheryl admitted later to feeling a little hurt that I didn't shed a tear. What we knew and Cheryl didn't was that her sister Lesley was having a surprise farewell party the following night. Tears aplenty after that occasion!

CHAPTER 19

BATTLE HARDENED

After the holiday in Jersey we resumed our fight with the Local Education Authority to get Matthew into Alresford School, this time as a full time pupil. The L.E.A. agreed in principle but, of course, as usual it all came down to money. They were reluctant to fund full time support. Once again we enlisted the help of our MP Sir Anthony Buck and with his invaluable support the LEA capitulated and agreed to fund two posts.

Matthew would have one helper for lesson times and an additional helper to cover the lunch period. We were very fortunate that the two ladies appointed proved to be sensitive and supportive.

Another hurdle had been cleared but it raised more difficulties with our success. Whilst Matthew was attending Thomas Wolsey his physio and speech therapies were catered for but now he had left we had to find an alternative. Having fought so hard to get Matthew into Alresford full time I was very reluctant to take him out of school a day per week and make appointments for him in Colchester. The speech therapists were now of the view that Matthew's speech had reached full potential so they felt further therapy was unlikely to be of any benefit.

Physiotherapy however was always ongoing and his exercises needed to be monitored and adjusted as he grew. Stretching exercises I could always do but we would also need guidance and advice in the future, especially with practical equipment.

Another battle commenced. Referring to each episode as a battle may seem melodramatic to folk that have no experience with disabled children, but trust me that is exactly how it is. Nobody comes knocking on your door to inform you of services available or where to go for help and advice, and we were more fortunate than most because we had friends with a disabled daughter who had trodden a similar path before us.

Barry and I are not naturally aggressive or demanding people, but we learnt early on that to get the best for Matthew it was a fight and we had to stand our ground, something that has become ingrown in Matthew. During such battles you are on your own and every step is a soul search and is demanding of your physical and mental strength. At this point I have to reiterate how fortunate we were to be surrounded by wonderful family and friends, but even with all that support you can still feel isolated.

We found a private physiotherapist who was experienced at working with children with CP. The downside to this arrangement was that, as Matthew grew and needed equipment such as wheelchairs, we would not qualify to get them on the NHS. I felt very aggrieved about this, we were both taxpayers and had already worked so hard with Matthew it seemed so unfair.

As luck would have it there was light at the end of the tunnel in the form of Jan Compton, Senior Paediatric community physiotherapist. She was a diminutive person but a real tough cookie. Jan proposed visiting Matthew once a fortnight after school and in time she became a good friend and close ally to us all. Her quick wit and ever-ready humour was exactly the right foil to motivate Matthew. Matthew's determination and wicked sense of humour cemented a mutual admiration society that still exists today.

I have asked Nikki to include some of her memories and Jan coming to visit and work with Matt is one she has flagged up.

It transpires that Nikki felt most aggrieved that during Matt's sessions with Jan, she was always told to go and play in the garden.

CHAPTER 20

IF AT FIRST YOU DON'T SUCCEED

Matthew was trying so hard with his walking. His legs were painfully thin and looked too weak to support his weight but Matthew being Matthew just persevered and practiced at every opportunity. Jan concentrated on teaching Matthew how to get up on his feet unaided.

"Nose over toes" was her much repeated instruction! With his usual grim determination he mastered this skill over a period of time, but for you to get the full picture I need to explain how he managed to achieve it. First he got into a kneeling position. Once kneeling he got his right foot forward and putting his weight and balance through this he gritted his teeth and "launched" himself forward and upwards. To get upright might take many attempts but once he was up on his toes he had to keep moving as it was the momentum that kept him there! His momentum not always taking him where he wanted to go! Sometimes he just spun around on the spot before he could aim for his intended destination. As soon as he stopped moving down he went.

As I have already described his legs were terribly thin so each attempt looked painful rather than elegant but again and again he tried, with us holding our breath and willing him to succeed.

Gradually the distance between falls got longer as his technique and confidence improved. Looking back at videos taken at this time it really was a heart stopping achievement. All that effort and us shouting at him to get his heels down! Despite all the injuries and setbacks never was anybody more determined to walk and of course reach his ultimate ambition to kick a football. Matthew loved the game and was spurred on by the knowledge that his dad had once been a professional footballer.

Matthew never tired or missed an opportunity to kick a ball. We put up small goal posts in the garden and when Barry wasn't around he persuaded anybody and everybody to play football with him.

Poignantly Barry could see that despite his disabilities Matthew had a very good eye for the ball and could have made an excellent goalkeeper. Dribbling and sweating from all the effort he had used, covered in mud, and invariably blood, he was certainly a sight to behold coming in from the garden after a session of football. You had more chance of raising the Titanic than stopping him play. As you can imagine he went through trousers like there was no tomorrow. I invented all manner of ways in which to patch trousers, and it was a good job I was handy with a needle and thread. We couldn't believe the state of his poor leather-like knees but he just carried on regardless!

One of Matthew's biggest fans was our neighbour, Wally. Wally was a surrogate granddad to both children. He used to come over to the fence and cheer Matthew on, keeping a careful check on how many steps Matthew had managed. Wally's favourite phrase was, "He'll do it; he'll get there". Many times he would turn away with tears in his eyes. His belief in Matthew was unshakeable.

Back to physio, and not intending this to be biased, Jan used to video tape Matthew's activities. She not only used the footage to monitor Matthew's progress but also for training, studying CP and inspiring other children and their parents.

When Matthew was about nine years old we heard about the Peto Institute in Hungary. It was founded by Andras Peto and worked purely with children suffering from Cerebal Palsy. Their methods were called

Conductive Education and their results were phenomenal. The programme involved intensive and repetitive exercises carried out by a "conductor". Each child followed their own individual programme every day, seven days a week. Some of the exercises looked very extreme and included sleeping on wooden slats. We watched several videos and discussed it with Jan. As I said, some of the results were phenomenal. Children who were immobile to begin with were, after months of this intensive programme, able to stand and walk.

Should Matthew, Nikki and I apply to go on this programme? Leave Barry behind and go and live in Hungary? After a great deal of debate we decided against it, and for the following reasons.

It would mean leaving Barry behind for months on end and the strain on family life was already well documented. Matthew would miss out on the love and support from our close family and friends. This had come to mean so much and had been invaluable to his life so far. It was also very unfair to Nikki. I could not bear to leave her behind, but once in Hungary life would have to revolve around Matthew and the programme.

Matthew's age was against him; ideally they worked with children from a very early age. We decided it was too high a price to pay. Matthew was motivated and making extremely good progress with traditional methods.

I believe Conductive Education is now widely used in this country.

Frequently throughout Matthew's early years I was approached by various trainee professionals. They wanted to use Matthew as a case study or as part of the research they were conducting. I never refused because I felt the more study and research that went on the more likelihood of help in the future. I was also asked by many professionals to speak to new parents who had just found themselves in our situation. Always happy to oblige, there is nothing more useful than talking to someone else in the same boat and, more importantly, someone to listen with understanding ears.

I did however find it frustrating on occasions when self-pity prevented people from helping themselves and their child. Matt wasn't in this category and explains here:

Matt:

DANGLE THAT CARROT

Physiotherapists to me, are the most evil but some of the most helpful people on the planet! Evil, because they enjoy making you go through torture but helpful as without them you would not improve! Jan was one of my angels, dressed as the devil and I owed a great deal to her constant nagging and her famous quote "nose over toes!" Even though I hated physio, I understood the reason and, because of mine and my family's desire for me to walk, I kept going. That and my competitive nature! I feel adamantly that people with cerebral palsy have an extra competitive brain cell which can be the key to overcoming obstacles such as walking. It worked for me as I was never content with the number of steps I walked and so would have to try and raise the bar.

Although, I do not recall knowing about the possibility of moving to Hungary I can safely say, in hindsight, my parents, like most occasions, made the right decision as I would never want to be the reason for such upheaval and cannot imagine being away from Dad and family, so thank you. Although, we would have had loads of ghoulash!

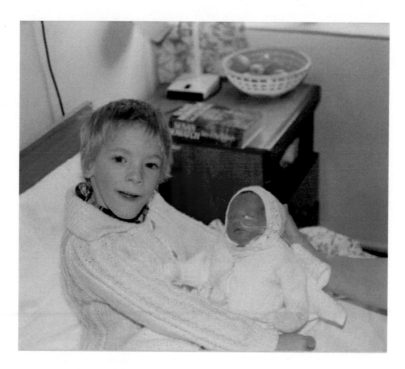

A very BIG and Proud BRO holds a very tiny Nikki

Butter wouldn't melt in their mouths: a school photo from 1991

Barry and Matt with the Pony that Barry had run the London Marathon to raise the funds for in 1989

Nanny Tiney and Grandad George at Matt's cousin Claire's Wedding

Matt and Nikki at the "Theatre of Dreams;" Old Trafford in 1992 on the unofficial tour!

Want a lift little sister?

Matthew was trying so hard with his walking. His legs were painfully thin and looked too weak to support his weight but Matthew being Matthew just persevered and practised at every opportunity.

One of the biggest days of his life: Matt meets his idol
Ryan Giggs at Norwich City in 1992

Not Lewis Hamilton
but Matt driving a
go-kart at Jean and
Rogers' Summer of 1991

CHAPTER 21

OUR AMERICAN DREAM

On a very cold grey January morning in 1990 Barry and I went to the travel agents to book a holiday.

In July we were off to Cincinnati to spend two weeks with Cheryl and Alan. I rang Cheryl to let her know the holiday was booked. We were so excited laughing and crying all at the same time. Cheryl and I were very regular correspondents and I still managed to bend her ear about all our trials and tribulations, but it wasn't the same as having her close at hand. On special occasions such as Christmas, New Year and birthdays we had chats on the phone which were great but never long enough. At long last July came round and our departure date arrived.

Mum and Dad were installed to house and pet sit and we set off for Gatwick. Neither of us had been to the States before so it was doubly exciting. The flight seemed very long and by the time we arrived at Cincinnati airport we were exhausted. Immigration seemed to take forever and a day, but once through Immigration and out into Arrivals the tiredness and frustration were forgotten as we saw the Baxter family anxiously scanning the crowds for us. We hadn't seen them for such a long time, it was magic all talking, laughing, hugging and shaking hands at once. The boys had grown so much and had developed American accents!

Cheryl and Alan drove us back to their beautiful home in Lamplite Court and we started a truly wonderful holiday. We had hired a car for the duration of our holiday and the next day Cheryl drove us to the hire centre. The car we were allocated was a Buick Skylark Automatic.

After completing the formalities it was agreed that Barry would follow Cheryl and the family back to Lamplite Court. As Cheryl drove off ahead of Barry it suddenly occurred to him that in addition to driving on the "wrong side of the road", he hadn't got Cheryl and Alan's address or even phone number! Talk about pressure for him to make sure he kept up with her. Of course this was way before mobile phones and sat-nav! Luckily he didn't lose her.

Nintendo had just become the latest craze in the States. Andrew and Paul had one so Matthew was introduced to its wonders and life has never been the same since! Christopher was the very proud owner of a battery operated jeep and against his better judgment was persuaded to let Nikki drive it. Big mistake! She was so busy waving to us and not looking where she was going that she hit the side of the house and dented a beautiful friendship. Christopher has since forgiven her but she will never be allowed to forget it.

During our second week Barry and I took Matthew and Nikki to Niagara Falls. We spent three days in Niagara stopping off in Cleveland en route to visit "Sea World." Niagara Falls is spectacular especially when lit at night. To get the best view you need to go up to the top of the Skylon Tower, or so Barry informed me! What he had failed to mention was that you go up in an elevator situated on the outside of the tower; not the most attractive prospect for someone suffering from vertigo! Once at the top you get out of the lift and walk around and, even for someone with no head for heights, the views are amazing looking down over the Falls.

"Bunny" had his usual holiday photo shoot! We really enjoyed our few days in Niagara but were ready to return to our Cincinnati home.

After a twelve-hour drive it was great to be with the Baxter family again. They were the perfect hosts and just occasionally Cheryl and I managed to draw breath.

Matthew particularly enjoyed the evenings and the football matches with the neighbourhood children. Because it was so hot during the daytime the children tended to stay inside and take advantage of the air conditioning, then coming out to play in the evenings when the temperature dropped. Barry and Alan were like magnets, for as soon as they went outside to kick a football around children appeared from all directions with Matthew taking up his favourite position as goalie.

Up until now Nikki will tell you she has few regrets in life but the first occurred in Cincinnati. Alan had tickets for Barry, Matthew and me to go to a baseball game. Their "local" team, the Cincinnati Reds, were playing the San Diego Padres.

Nikki was staying home with Cheryl, the boys and also Victoria, Cheryl's niece visiting for the summer. They had a special treat planned for Nikki. This particular evening they were going to catch fireflies, lightning bugs. These bugs glow in the dark and Children catch them and put them in jars to use as lanterns. It was great fun, an unrepeatable experience.

Unfortunately though as Nikki was only three years old, she didn't know Cheryl all that well and as far as she was concerned, she had just been deserted by her entire family! After we left for the baseball game Nikki was inconsolable, eventually crying herself to sleep long before it got dark and the fireflies appeared! Cheryl was upset she hadn't been able to comfort Nikki and to this day Nikki wishes she could turn back the clock.

Nikki and Cheryl, I am very pleased to say are now very close and have often laughed about that night. Incidentally we had a great time at the baseball. The "Reds" won.

Our two weeks went all too quickly and it was time to come home. I had kept a diary of our holiday and a passage from the last day reads,

I gave Cheryl strict instructions not to cry when we leave as I definitely won't.

"No problem," says Cheryl. "I'm hardened to saying goodbye." Our flight was called and, well, we had both lied!

Matt:

THE CINCINNATI NESS MONSTER!

I have fond memories of this holiday, not only for my introduction to the Nintendo and Teenage Mutant Ninja Turtles, but it was our first time in America. Mum and Dad had been so excited to go and see Cheryl and Alan, as were Nik and I but we did not know what to expect. Although I cannot remember the whole holiday vividly, quite a few memories stand out and I shall share some with you here.

The first memory has to be my introduction to Nintendo. No, not the SNES (Super Nintendo) but the NES! Cheryl and Alan's three boys Andrew, Paul and Chris have been friends of mine all my life, well maybe not Chris as he's Nik's age. I had been so looking forward to seeing the Baxters, especially Andrew and Paul, and so when they showed me the wonders of the NES our time was largely spent playing on it, including Duck Hunt and Super Mario and of course Turtles. Now, I had never played on a games console before so it took me a little while to figure out how to use the control pad but eventually I used my right hand and right knee (hard to imagine I know). Anyway, I should thank the boys for letting me bash the buttons with my knee, your faces were a picture! I'm not too sure who enjoyed the NES more, the children or the adults, but all I know is we got a NES soon after the holiday and there grew Mum and Dad's affinity for Double Dragon!

The weather most days was scorching, heat which I'd never experienced before, and so doing stuff during the day was an effort (says I who was in my push chair a lot), well it looked like an effort! Anyway, the evenings were my favourite time of day as we had quite a few barbecues at which Alan and Dad did the typical male thing and stood cooking the meat whilst drinking plenty of Mich's (Michelob's). We boys and Nik used to get the football out in the back field and within ten minutes children and their dads from the neighbourhood came and we, of course, had football matches. Yes of course I claimed my usual position between the two jumpers laid on the floor as goals. The matches were highly amusing because Dad and Alan added some competitiveness to them, usually making them Brits versus Americans. I think those matches are where Nik's competitive streak comes from, and mine too for that matter!

Another good memory was of Coney Island theme park. I am sure Nik will not appreciate me sharing this but hey ho it always makes me smile. We went on a ride (can't remember the theme) but it was for young children and towards the end there was an enormous head saying "Don't be scared, don't be scared" at which point Nikki freaked out and it took her years to get over that (sorry Sis).

Another memory starring Nikki was when she was eventually allowed to drive Chris's electric ride-on jeep. It took us days to try and persuade him to let Nikki have a go and when he did she crashed it into the side of the house! Suffice to say she never drove it again. However, a kiss on the cheek made up for it!

While we were at the Baxter's, so too was Victoria, as Mum has mentioned. We all got along famously and, because she was older than us, she was put in charge of child-minding duties a couple of times. Now, in Cincinnati at about 8pm at night, fireflies come out and are amazing to see, especially when children catch them in jars and they look like lanterns. Well, Nikki had always wanted to go out with the children to catch them but was always in bed by the time it was firefly catching time. So one night Alan managed to get tickets to see the Cincinnati Reds take on San Diego Padres in baseball, so he took my parents and me to the game. I must admit,

106

despite it being an amazing experience, I did not have a clue what was going on. Apparently the Reds won!

Meanwhile, Cheryl had promised Nikki that while we were at baseball, she and Victoria would take her firefly catching as that was the one thing she had really really wanted to do all holiday, but that night Nik would not stop crying and so did not go firefly catching!

As well as some great memories of our holiday I must mention my introduction to 'chilli dogs', that is sausages in chilli sauce and covered in batter. The Baxter's love them but, without sounding ungrateful, they are the most revolting thing I have ever eaten and have never tried since!

And you're still trying to picture me using the controller, I bet!

CHAPTER 22

SPOOKY EXPERIENCE AND A FISHY TALE

I can't remember the exact year; Nikki was about three or four so Matthew nine or ten. We had booked an Autumn half-term break in Lyme Regis in Dorset. Barry and I were looking forward to showing the children where we had lived when we first got married. The hotel we had booked was very old, and just a short walk through some woods behind the hotel and you were straight onto the beach. John Fowles, author of The Collector and The French Lieutenant's Woman lived very close by. The "Cobb" very integral to the story of The French Lieutenant's Woman is the heart of Lyme Regis. It was a perfect location and very atmospheric!

Our bedroom was very large, and off this room, down two steps into an alcove was the old dressing room which now contained bunk beds and this is where Matthew and Nikki slept. Through French windows ran a long balcony. The windows were locked at that time of the year. As you would expect the floorboards creaked their age as you walked across them. Immediately below our room was Reception and beside that the hotel lounge and bar.

There was an intercom in our room connected to the reception desk below and this meant that Barry and I could go down to the bar in the evening after the children had gone to sleep. Matthew was perfectly happy about this arrangement. He knew what to do if either of them wanted us for It was no different from us being downstairs at home. After a long and busy day both children were asleep by about 9.30pm. One particular evening Barry and I switched on the intercom and went down to the bar. We were chatting to the hotel owner and fellow guests when the lady on reception walked through and did a double take to see Barry and me sitting there.

"Oh you are both here" she said. "I have just been listening and heard footsteps walking around your room." Before she could finish Barry and I raced upstairs. Both children were fast asleep, the windows still locked, there was nobody there! Later we were told by the hotel staff this frequently happens. The story goes like this. The hotel was believed to be haunted by an old lady; she patrolled the hotel checking the rooms where children were sleeping alone. Just making sure all was well. It was years later we told Matthew and Nikki the story. They hadn't heard or felt a thing that night.

It was during this holiday that Matthew suffered one of the first of his very frequent and violent Migraine attacks. We had all enjoyed a large cooked breakfast before heading off to visit the Sealife Centre in Weymouth. We stopped off along the way to show Matthew and Nikki our old home. We had a quick visit to our old friends and neighbours.

Once we arrived in Weymouth Matthew was not feeling too bright but said he was okay to carry on. We walked around the large pools in the Sea Life centre admiring all the marine life. Large sting rays coming up to the surface to wave hello. It was fascinating though slightly pungent!

There was one more building to visit. This one contained the baby fish from all the exotic species they had been breeding. The walkways were above the tanks so you looked down into all the teeming pools. I was slowly pushing Matthew's chair along the elevated walkways making sure he didn't miss anything, when suddenly he was the victim of the most violent, projectile vomiting I have ever witnessed.

Poor Matthew, lucky fish hungrily snapping up this unexpected snack! It was awful but has since become one of Matthew's favourite anecdotes in the league of disgusting tales! Unfortunately the migraines have yet to swim away. Matthew goes on:

Matt:

SPOOK DELIGHT AND FISHY FRIGHT

Ever since I can remember I have been fascinated with the paranormal, ghosts and spirits and thinking about it, the ghostly babysitter was probably the catalyst. In any case, it is a lovely story and the kind which is the reason for my belief. It seems, in many ghost stories, that when you die, you suddenly become an evil spirit, wreaking havoc but to me that is not the case. I have had many experiences where the spirit has been just as lovely as it was in life, such as Granddad George, my soul mate in life and now guardian after life. This is just what I believe but I would never try and to push it onto anyone.

However having a nice ghostly babysitter is pretty cool. Fortunately, due to my migraine, I do not recall much about my infamous aquarium feeding but do remember the overpowering stench of fish and the feeding frenzy which ensued! Not one of my most glorious days but definitely one to share!

CHAPTER 23

THE PRICE OF INDEPENDENCE

Matthew was settling very well into Alresford School, making friends and generally being accepted as just one of the kids. However what was becoming very clear to us was his inability to get around independently. Yes it was all very well being able to walk and fall in his garden but beyond this he needed support. By now he had outgrown his "Pickle" and other toys on the market were too small and babyish.

We needed to investigate more specialised modes of mobility. Most of his peers were walking to school, going to the local shop and park unaccompanied and of course Matthew wanted to do the same.

After a bit of research we discovered the "Pony". A battery operated, motorised scooter built by a company in Wisconsin USA. It had a top speed of 8mph and could go up to 16 miles on one charge. Absolutely perfect. The only problem was the price - £1760. We had some serious fundraising to do.

Using his natural talents Barry entered the London Marathon and we hoped to raise the money in sponsorship. The local BBC radio station was told of our goal and they came to do an interview. The response was staggering. I wrote to every sponsor thanking them at the time but, if any of you are reading this, then THANK you again.

Local clubs, organisations, businesses, neighbours, children, pensioners, family and friends all got behind us pledging their support. Even the Paediatricians looking after Matthew sponsored Barry. Some of the pledges were as small as 20p but every penny counted and was appreciated.

No pressure then! All Barry had to do was run 26.2 miles.

Training was hard and anyone attempting to run the London marathon deserves total respect and admiration. The longest and most arduous training is done in the bleakest months of the year. Unfortunately Barry contracted bronchitis and his training was severely impaired throughout January and February. It looked doubtful whether he would be fit enough to compete but we had reckoned without the care and support of Dr Snell. He was determined to get Barry fit enough to run and he did.

The day finally came and a large group of us went to London to cheer Barry on. The atmosphere in London on marathon day is brilliant, the crowds are so supportive, and so, despite cramp and injury, Barry crossed the finish line in 4hrs 23mins.

The money rolled in and we reached our target. The Pony was ordered and paid for. Then we waited and waited. Every delivery date promised by the company's agents in Ireland passed. The disappointment and frustration were unbearable.

In desperation I contacted BBC Essex again. After a follow up interview the original reporter contacted the company in Wisconsin and within a week the Pony arrived. The power of the BBC!

Words alone cannot describe the difference this little machine made to Matthew's life. Orange, black and silver with sheepskin seat covers, it looked a very cool machine. Locally there was no limit. The school caretaker built a shelter beside Matthew's classroom to house it whilst he was in school. Going to school, Cubs, the park, shops, walking the dogs, visiting friends all under his own steam made Matthew a very familiar sight in and around Alresford. Being easy to dismantle we were able to take it on family trips.

Nikki remembers getting into "scrapes" as she describes it, when at the park another child would covet Matt's Pony and take it for a spin!

Woe betide any child that tried this trick whilst Nikki was around! Matt recalls:

MY NOBLE STEED

First and foremost, I must say a massive thank you to those who donated money for my scooter and of course to Dad for doing the marathon. Having the scooter gave me independence, (as well as a few bruises), which I'd never had before. Before my parents decided to fundraise, Thomas Wolsey School kindly lent me an old scooter in order for us to find out if I was capable of using one. The borrowed scooter was old and covered in dust but I was so excited when we brought it home after school one Friday night. All day at school I was excited to get on my new mode of transport, so when I finally got home you can imagine my disappointment when I got on it and it wouldn't move! The battery charger was not working! Probably down to months of inactivity. Dad spent all that Saturday morning trying to get a replacement battery or charger but without success.

It is here where I must admit to possessing a temper and, while it may be easy to say, it was a result of frustration, I feel I must apologise to anyone who bore the brunt of it. Possessing the knowledge of my temper. I return your attention to the scooter which didn't work - **didn't** being the operative word.

That Saturday afternoon mum, dad, nanny and granddad were out in the garden, and I went out to the garage to sit on the lifeless scooter, wishing it to work but it didn't, so what does one do when something doesn't work and all engineering answers fail? You give it a kick! This is exactly what I did and guess what..............it went beep! The fix-it kick worked! I drove it out of the garage and into the garden, which was no mean feat considering the narrow doorways and pavement. Mum and Dad were amazed. Their faces were a picture! It was obvious pretty much straight away what it would mean having my own scooter and so fundraising got underway.

Now, after a few weeks of having the borrowed scooter and enjoying the freedom it gave me, Thomas Wolsey needed it back for a new student so my anticipation for my own one was increased hundred fold! So, when Dad fell ill I feared the worst, no marathon, no sponsor money and ultimately no scooter. I am aware that I sound selfish and, in some cases, I regret to say I was, but it was like getting a new toy and being allowed to play with it for a day and then having it put somewhere out of reach but in full view.

Fortunately, and with my eternal gratitude, Dad did the marathon and I was so proud of him and humbled by all the sponsors. You can imagine how excited I was to hear Dad had raised enough money for my scooter! As Mum mentioned, the delivery date kept being put back and, although being disappointed, I could see it was upsetting my parents so I tried to forget about it. Then BBC Essex, who I need to thank, got involved and put pressure on the scooter company and a week or so later my noble steed arrived – Happy days! Thinking about it now, I think that was when my interest in journalism started.

I realize this is a long piece but I feel I should share this funny anecdote with you. I was riding home from school one day on my scooter and our house was on the main road going into the village and it was common to have a policeman with a speed gun monitoring the cars. Anyway, this one day, the policeman pointed the speed gun at me and jokingly said "I'll have to arrest you for speeding, you're doing six miles an hour!" to which I replied, "You'll have to catch me first!" I wonder how many people on mobility scooters have been arrested for speeding? (Best Google it!)

CHAPTER 24

LOCKS AND MARATHONS

Matthew's sense of fun and devil-ment on one particular occasion almost finished me off. Is this me being over dramatic again? Please judge for yourself.

The Nottingham Marathon, held every September, was one of our favourite weekends of the year. Alan and Ann's very good friends John and Dee Kitchin live in Nottingham with their three children Helen, Annette and Damien. Each year, together with Alan and Ann's family, we invaded the Kitchin home for the marathon weekend.

John, Dee and family made the weekend all run like clockwork. It was shopping for the girls on Saturday afternoon and Nottingham Forest football match for the boys.

Barry:

FOOTBALL AT FOREST

Most people were brilliant with Matt and helped as best they could. However we met the odd "prats" two of whom were a steward and a policeman at Forest's city ground for a match against Arsenal. They insisted on operating a one-way system to our seats. Our seats were two places from one end of a row but they made us traverse about 90 seats to get to our places instead of allowing us to go in at the other end. Alan and friend John were murderous over the JOBSWORTH attitudes of these two Muppets!

Another "little Hitler" incident occurred in Ipswich town centre when we had to attend an assessment appointment in their lovely town. They were really unpleasant, obstructive and totally unhelpful, when all we were asking was for some advice about where to park! Fortunately "Prats" like these were truly a minority.

The house was divided into dormitories to accommodate all the sleeping bodies.

Sunday was the marathon day. We were up with the lark, breakfast eaten and packed lunches made then off to Victoria embankment for the start of the race giving Alan, Barry and Melvyn a good send off.

As soon as the runners were off we started our own "Supporters marathon". We sped off to our first cheer point in Lentern lane about 10 miles into the run. Our second spot was Radcliffe Road, which was the 15 mile mark and close enough to John and Dee's house for a very short comfort break. Our next cheer spot was at the 21mile mark, At this point the going is really tough and the runners need all the encouragement they can get! Then finally back to Victoria Park and the Finish.

Runners safely collected, it was back to the Kitchin home for one of Dee's legendary casserole dinners before the long drive back to Essex. Wonderful fun, crazy times enveloped in the very warm Kitchin family hospitality.

To return to the tale of Matthew's 'daring do' on his scooter.

Part of the marathon encompassed the National Water sport centre at Holme Pierpoint. One Saturday afternoon we decided to go and have a look round. There are lots of lock gates and one in particular has a very steep drop. Matthew of course was on his scooter and mischief getting the better of him he decided to have a closer look at this lock, a much closer look!

He drove to the very edge and skidded to a halt. Just one involuntary movement and all that effort and fundraising would have been wasted!

116

"Mummy's special little soldier" is not what I called him on that occasion!

Some weeks later our roles were reversed and I almost managed to finish him off completely. We were having our Sunday dinner of roast beef, when I made a remark that made Matt laugh just as he was swallowing a piece of beef. He started to choke, lips turning blue! I was, I am ashamed to say, too panicked to respond. Thankfully Barry was far more quick thinking, he got behind Matt and performed the "Heimlich manoeuvre". The meat shot out of Matt's mouth, his colour and breathing restored. From that day Barry claims Matt owes him his life!

BARRY:

I clearly remember that day! It definitely was Sunday lunchtime, a tradition in our household; the roast; and it was Wendy's lovely beef this particular time. Matt was around ten years old and had just put a piece of beef into his mouth when Wendy made him laugh. Bad move; he promptly inhaled the meat and started choking! To this day I don't know how I knew what to do in this instance. Back then it was called the "Heimlich manoeuvre". I performed an abdominal thrust and thankfully up popped the offending piece of meat, much to our relief and especially a very guilty feeling Mum.

Ever since that day I have teased Matt that I own him body, soul and mind! Apparently this is the case when a Native American Indian saves someone's life!!

You may have noticed that Matthew has now become Matt. I can't remember exactly when we were informed by Matt of his change of identity.   He felt "Matthew" was not cool and "Matty" as he was very fondly called by most folk was now too babyish. The only exception he made to being called Matty was his beloved Grandma. So there you have it. For the purposes of this book the start of a "New" life is as good a place as any!

CHAPTER 25

A HOLIDAY AND A BEREAVMENT

In 1991 my mum, Tiney, had a heart attack and rapidly became a very poorly lady. She was in constant pain with severe rheumatoid arthritis but had always put a brave face on it. The heart attack however seemed to defeat her and she lost her sparkle. Sadly Nikki's memories of her nanny are mostly associated with nanny's bad health whereas Matthew's memories are very different. Nanny had always been a fun play mate when Matt was little and a good listener as he got older.

That year we had booked a holiday in Minorca, but a few days before we were due to leave Tiney developed a thrombosis and was rushed into hospital. Both mum and dad insisted we still go away, my sister Jean came to stay with dad and give her support with the promise that dad would let us know if mum's condition worsened. We set off for Minorca.

It was Matt's first break from his "Pony" so his independence was going to be severely curtailed. He had three options:

- Crawl everywhere, undignified and impractical.
- Be pushed in his buggy, not the coolest way to be seen.
- Walk with our help.

All three options were unattractive and underlined just how much his Pony had changed his life. We all knew whatever we did would attract unwanted attention and stares, but we all had fairly thick skins by now.

From experience children will be curious about Matt and then mostly accepting. But there will always be one child who is unkind, usually in a very sneaky way, and Minorca was no exception.

Once again Matt's champion, now aged four and a force to be reckoned with dealt with the culprit in her own sweet way!

What self-respecting teenager is going to admit he was pushed fully clothed into the swimming pool by a tiny Disney clad toddler!

NIKKI RECALLS:

HOLIDAY TIMES

I'm lucky in that I have so many fond memories of our family holidays. Every summer mum and dad made sure we had a fortnight of quality family time. They worked very hard for it, only now do I appreciate how hard.

One of the earliest holidays that I remember was Minorca. Aside from the ant-infested room, it is really the first summer holiday I have a clear recollection of.

There was a massive swimming pool full of other "playmates", a beautiful sandy beach, where dad, Matt and I spent hours sculpting with damp sand: we made castles, forts, dams and Matt would bury me. Matt and I would splash about in the rock pools. Matt spent most of his time on his knees, which were basically his leather soled shoes at this time.

Another reason this holiday springs to mind is because it's the first time I consciously remember sticking up for my big brother. I'm told my "boxing career" started long before but I was too young to remember.

There was an older boy, about Matt's age, who started mimicking him by the pool. I don't remember the exact events but I know that it continued into the evening entertainment. I recall the boy standing by the swimming pool. He had wavy dark brown hair worn in the "curtain style," and I clearly remember Matt wearing a vibrant multi-coloured baseball cap, which I really wanted! I had now had quite enough of this bully's behavior and so I strolled over to him and gave him a mighty shove. He was twice my age and size but he fell into the pool splashing and coughing and fully clothed! I remember Mum and Dad trying hard not to laugh as his mother, who had ignored her son's ignorant behaviour, hauled him out. We didn't apologise!

This holiday was my first experience of being laughed at by other people and so my first taster of what it could feel like to be in Matt's shoes. There was a fancy dress competition, Matt was a pirate and I was dressed up as "Noddy". Mum and Dad had done a great job with our costumes and we really looked the part.

We had to line up on the stage in our costumes and in turn say who we were and where we came from. Without mummy or daddy there to hold your hand it was very daunting for a four year old. Of course being only four I hadn't yet grasped the concept of coming from England and so I told the Minorcan host I was from Alresford, confusing her completely! It got even worse when I told her I was Noddy to which she replied "Notty, who is Notty?" It appears although Noddy is well known in England they had never heard of him in Minorca! The audience broke into fits of laughter and I burst into tears!

Our hotel was situated a little way out of town. However the nearest part of the town was just over the hill and made for a very pleasant evening stroll. We wandered in most evenings to have a meal and look at the shops etc. Because of the town's geography most of the shops were built on the side of the hill and reached by long low steps.

Just for fun, Barry decided one evening to run up the steps pushing Matt in his buggy and then for the hell of it run down pretending to be out of control. The joke went over my head. As I saw it Matt was hurtling toward the road, so being a quick thinking and caring mum I stuck my foot out to stop the speeding chariot. As Matt sailed past my eyes I realised in horror he was not strapped in! I watched in absolute disbelief as he bumped down the steps and finally came to a stop at the bottom. We raced to him and as I turned him over and gasped at his grazed face and knees he muttered those immortal words, "You have never liked me have you?"

Needless to say it is a story he has embroidered and dined out on many times. Little did he realise then there was so much more to come and not so very far away.

We had a brilliant two weeks without further mishap and as soon as we got back to Colchester we went straight to the hospital to visit Nanny. What a transformation! Her sparkle was back and even the arthritis in her hands that had plagued her for so many years was much better.

After our visit we went back to the car and Matt suddenly burst into tears. I thought it was some kind of relief hysteria, a reaction to Nanny's new found health. Being that caring mum again I hugged him and patted him on the back telling him Nanny was going to be fine. But this only made him cry more and so I hugged him tighter and patted him harder. Then from amongst the sobs an indignant voice "There's a bloody wasp in my shirt!" Taking its revenge on Matt for all my motherly concern!

Tiney continued to enjoy her good health throughout the summer until the end of September when once again she started to deteriorate.

As usual we were planning another Bonfire party, the date set for Saturday 2nd November. It was also going to be a birthday celebration for Matt.

Tiney was too poorly to come to the party so we visited her on the Friday. As it was Matt's birthday she made a supreme effort to disguise how ill she felt but she was clearly a very poorly lady.

That evening I cooked Matt's favourite meal, steak with all the trimmings. The phone rang at 10pm, it was dad to say Mum was much worse and could I get there as soon as possible? I arrived just five minutes after she had passed away in my dad's arms. Dad came back to our house that night and Nikki was delighted to find him there in the morning. Very gently we told her that Nanny had died to which she replied, "Oh good now Granddad can come to the party". Nanny would have loved that! The party went ahead and everyone drank a toast to Tiney.

Matt writes:

A FOND FAREWELL TO SOMEONE SPECIAL

It is never nice saying goodbye to someone you love. However, not getting the chance is even worse. Fortunately, I got the chance to say just that to Nanny, which I'm forever thankful for. Nanny was one of our rocks (even though she was tiny!) and as Mum has said, a great playmate. I remember many happy days spent at Nanny and Granddad's watching her cooking sausage and mash with baked beans whilst I was stirring blocks of soap in a mixing bowl. I'm not sure if Mum is aware of this, but when we visited Nanny the day before my birthday something inside me made me give her an extra big hug as we were leaving, and I said "Goodbye Nanny, I love you lots" to which she said the same. I am not sure how, as she was being brave, but I knew that was the last time I would see her.

As for Mum never liking me I shall leave it up to you to decide. However, I would like to recap, and so far Mum has caused me to:

- Choke

- Made me fly out of my buggy face first

- Caused me to be stung eleven times

AND THERE'S MORE TO COME!

CHAPTER 26

GRANDAD

Coming to terms with losing Tiney was very hard especially for my dad. For some years he had been caring for Tiney and now he found time hung heavy and the days were long and lonely without her.

He had always been a keen gardener and helped out in the gardens of a local old people's home. But despite this keeping him busy and having many friends he was clearly finding life quite empty.

Somebody suggested he join the "Care Network", as a driver, which he did and he soon became a very popular and busy driver. Taking elderly and disabled people to hospital appointments or shopping he was much in demand. Sadly his own health was deteriorating, a fact he had been able to hide whilst mum was alive.

After a couple of spells in Colchester Hospital he was transferred to the Royal London Hospital. We knew he was a very sick man but we hoped he would get well enough in London to be transferred back to the Hospice in Colchester.

During his time in the Royal London Dad forbade us to bring the children to see him. He didn't want them to see just how ill he looked and it wasn't the nicest and most respectful of environments. Patients with different religions to our own were treated in the same ward and their families were very disrespectful of the other patients. My dad was the most kind and tolerant person, his "religion" had always been "Do as you would be done by." His ethos, "If you can't say anything nice then don't say anything at all."

It upset me very much to see his peace and privacy so violated. He passed away three weeks later on August 8th just nine months after mum, and no matter what was on the death certificate I'm sure he died of a broken heart.

It took a long time for Matt and Nikki to understand that acting on Granddad's wishes I had to deny them the opportunity to say goodbye to him. His passing was a huge loss to all of us and most especially me. For all of my life he had been there, strong, caring, supportive and ever dependable. It took a long time for me to come to terms to life without him, but life does go on and I was to discover that selfish grief can be so destructive.

Matt's memories are:

TOUGH LOVE

People talk about a soul mate as someone who knows you inside out and who can cheer you up just by being there. Well to say Granddad George was my soul mate is an understatement. I am fortunate, I am close to every member of my family and consider myself as the luckiest guy ever. George and I did so much together and he was certainly my rock as I could tell him anything, and often did. He was the most optimistic and caring person I have ever known and it took me a long time to get over his passing. It is one of those cases where it was such a painful time for all of us that in order for me to support Mum and be 'big bro' to Nikki, I suppressed my feelings and shut it out. It was hard for me not being able to say goodbye to Granddad and I did feel angry for a long time. However, with time, I realize he and my Mum were right not to let us see him, but it was only twenty years later, with counselling that I truly dealt with his loss.

Now, many people will think it's wishful thinking or a load of old rubbish but due to my belief in the paranormal I believe George, along with others, is always by my side, a

126

belief which has been confirmed on more than one occasion, though I shall not disclose them as I could write a hundred pages on it. All I shall say is that for three different Mediums on three separate occasions to tell me what they did must be one almighty set up if not true!

CHAPTER 27

THE AFTERMATH OF LOSS

Nikki started school in September. She was so excited, especially as she would have her big brother there to look out for her. All appeared to be going well and then sadly our dog Sugar died unexpectedly in January.

I am ashamed to say that I was still wrapped up in my own grief at losing dad and I failed to notice what was happening to Nikki. At bed times we would have to go through certain routines before she would settle down to sleep. The last thing I had to do before kissing her goodnight was put my hands around her wrist to check her pulse. Of course I now know this is Obsessive Compulsive Disorder (OCD) but at the time it was just a nuisance.

Matters came to a head late one Saturday night when she woke up screaming with earache. Calpol didn't touch it so I rang the doctor's. The doctor said he would meet me at the surgery. He looked in her ears and discovered blue paper in them. When he questioned her about it she became hysterical, striking him and knocking everything off his desk. This behaviour was so bizarre and completely out of character.

Sunday morning saw us in the ENT department where they tried to remove everything from her ears but something was so firmly embedded it would require a general anaesthetic and surgery to extract it.

After her surgery we were told she had pushed so much into her ears that a stone had become so firmly embedded it may have damaged her eardrum. Nikki was referred to a Child Psychiatrist to try and discover why she had done this to herself.

At her first visit to the psychiatrist she would not even look at him. He told her, "That's okay. Perhaps you could draw a picture whilst I talk to your mum and dad". Nikki sat in the corner of his room with some felt tips and was soon engrossed in her drawing. When we had finished talking Nikki was quite happy to show the doctor her picture. She had drawn green grass and blue sky. In the middle of her picture there was a hill with a castle on top. Inside the castle was a person, and Nikki explained it was Matt.

The doctor assured us that although it was going to take a little time all would be well, and perhaps Matt would come to the next appointment. With Matt there at the next appointment Nikki was more forthcoming. Gentle questioning, teasing and making her laugh soon helped our little girl talk about her bewildering feelings and emotions.

Nikki felt guilty because she was not disabled. Two people she loved very much had died and then of course our dog, Sugar. To Nikki this wasn't fair, so she thought if she hurt herself no one else would die and she would be like Matt.

After the earaches started she got worried she was going to die and so all the night time routines were her way of reassuring herself she was ok. We were horrified, our little girl was troubled and frightened and we hadn't noticed. I felt so guilty. On reflection there had been two occasions when she had tried to tell me. Once she told me some blue paper had fallen into her ear, I looked but couldn't see anything so told her not to be so silly!! The second time I got a phone call from school asking me to go and get her as she was so upset and couldn't tell anyone why. Her behaviour was so out of character and hysterical the Headmaster told me he hadn't witnessed anything like it in all his years of teaching.

I took her to the doctor who couldn't find anything wrong and suggested it was probably just a "day mare". We came home, I gave her some Calpol and she eventually became calmer. It now transpires she had confided to her friend about putting paper in her ears and they told her she would have a tree growing in her ear.

Poor Nikki! With the psychiatrist's help we were eventually able to overcome her fears and then tackle the OCD behaviours.

Nikki's class teacher and Headmaster were very supportive, making her a "star chart". Each morning she went into school and if she had managed not to go through one of her routines at bedtime she got a star put on her chart. A whole week's worth of stars meant a reward.

We treated each routine the same way until finally they all stopped. Her ultimate reward was a Take That cassette!

Our little girl was back to her usual self and I had had a very loud wake up call. Being a parent of a disabled child is challenging but being a sibling can also be very tough and that must never be forgotten.

I would like to include some of Nikki's own words:

I'm not sure how old I was when I really realized my brother was different, because as I'm sure any sibling with a disabled brother or sister will tell you that person is just their brother or sister and nothing else.

At times I would find it difficult to understand when people would stare or make comments. Perhaps because I was blind to Matt's disability and, as he himself would tell you, out of everyone I understand his speech best. Often I used to get angry and frustrated when what was so clear to me was a daunting noise to another.

As mum has and Matt will explain we had a rough year as a family, Nanny, Granddad, Wally and Sugar died.

Being only five years old I do not remember much about this time but as mum has asked for some of my thoughts and recollections of my childhood memories I feel I should give my account of this period.

I know I was a confused child. Mortality was not a concept I had yet grasped and my confusion surrounding Matt's disability is clear. I did not understand why Matt was disabled and I was not!

Throughout my childhood I often felt guilty about this situation. Naively I believed that if I had been born first then Matt would be "normal" and so all of his problems were my fault and I felt guilty. This was a very difficult concept for a small child and it made me feel if I punished myself no one could hurt him or us.

When our loved ones died, I wanted to prevent anything else happening to my family. This is where my "OCD" commenced and, as Matt likes to call it, my "god phase". I was afraid of God and used to say a prayer obsessively every night, the words of which now elude me, but the rituals I had to perform included this prayer. My rituals were to prevent harm, as absurd as it now sounds. I was terrified of death and scared I would be punished for being born second. I would jump up and down on the spot until I could feel and hear my heart pounding, confirming to me I was very much alive. Sticking things in my ears to feel pain was, as I now understand it, part of my "punishment".

Every family has its own unique obstacles and problems, and I am not claiming my family is any different, except at the same time I am!

Death and grief are a part of life, and for me, as a very young child, this time was the icing on a very deep cake of confusion surrounding disability. Without it I do not think the loss of loved ones would have had the same effect and this is where our family is different from many others.

131

My mum had lost two of her foundations but had a young child and a disabled child to care for and so I feel my "Godphase" was inevitable.

To sum up, I think writing about this time is important to include because, even with the best childhood and a supportive family, being a sibling of a disabled child can be so hard at times, no matter how hard people try to compensate for it. I believe others will have difficulties in understanding "Why not me?"

My parents did talk to me about Matt's disabilities, but I wanted to try and emphasise from a child's view the deeper implications it can have on a family unit. With a lot of help, which mum has previously outlined, I came through the other side, a "Take That" tape the richer, more rounded and with better understanding of my confused feelings. It has held me in good stead even to this day. I find this period of my life embarrassing and difficult to reflect on, but it is a truthful and honest account from a sibling.

Matt continues:

SIBLING IN PAIN!

I must admit that this is the hardest part to write about. To know the people you care about the most are hurting and there is not anything you can say to fix them is gut wrenching, especially when you are part of the underlying factor.

I have said before that Nikki's arrival on this planet was the greatest gift I could ever wish for and she is the greatest person I know. Now, as Mum has mentioned, the year in which we lost Nanny, George and Sugar was the worst for all of us, especially Mum and Nikki. However, because we were extremely close and Nik reacted well to counseling we managed to come out the other side and although the pain of our loss still weighed heavily upon us all, with time it gradually eased, although they will never be forgotten.

I would like to lighten the mood a bit here as I tell you a funny story about Sugar our dog. I was about six or seven years old and one afternoon Mum and I noticed Sugar wasn't anywhere to be seen. After searching the house and garden thoroughly Mum rang Granddad and Nanny to come over to help us as Dad was at work. They soon arrived and at Mum's request Granddad took us in his car and drove around Alresford in search of our beloved Sugar. Whilst driving around we made people aware to keep a look out and pretty soon nearly the entire village was out searching for Sugar!

After a while of driving Granddad parked his car by a field full of sheep and said "Matt, look at those little lambs, aren't they cute", to which I sternly replied "Never mind the bloody lambs, what about Sugar!" Mum and Granddad found this amusing and even more so upon our return home. Dad had come home and found Sugar right as rain shut in the garage (the only place we didn't check!). Even to this day when we see lambs we think of Granddad and that Sugar hunt!

CHAPTER 28

BIG CHANGES

It was Matt's last year at primary school so big changes were ahead for him. Matt had loved being a pupil at Alresford School and had gained so much from his time there. We also like to think Matt made a valuable contribution to the school. The following poem was written by one of the teachers at the school, photos accompanied each verse:

MATTHEW OUR FRIEND

Matthew
Needs to be watched or,
Sooner or later he'll tyremark
your feet with his rollator.

Matthew
Needs to be watched or,
In his 'lectric scooter
He'll scare the pants off you
by blowing his hooter.

Matthew
Needs to be watched or,
While you are talking
He's stood up by himself
and gone off walking.

Matthew
Needs to be watched or,
Before lunchtime ends
You'll find he's chatted up

Six more girlfriends.

Matthew
Needs to be watched or,
Now he's growing stronger
It's hard to know where he is
Cos his "walks" are getting longer.

Matthew
Needs to be watched or,
Given half a chance
He'll have you running round the field
Be leading you a dance.

Matthew
Needs to be watched or,
Before you've a chance to shout
He's up on his feet and walking
Chasing the girls about.

Matthew
Needs to be watched or,
You'll miss the best moment of all
As Matthew climbs to his feet
And walks and kicks the ball.

Matthew
Needs to be watched
We have watched him and we've Cried,
To see him try and succeed
Fills your heart with pride.
Matthew
Needs to be watched
He'll get where he wants in the end
We're proud to be sharing his childhood
We're proud to be called his friends.

One chapter closes and another opens

CHAPTER 29

SECONDARY SCHOOL

The Headmaster of Alresford School, Mr Bob Newman, had always been very supportive and was determined Matt's transition to secondary school would be as smooth as possible. He arranged meetings between us and Mr McCrone, who was a deputy head at the local secondary school, the Colne Community school in Brightlingsea about four miles away. Mr McCrone was also incidentally head of the school's Maths department. I think it fair to say that at our first meeting Mr McCrone was not convinced Matt was a suitable student for his school.

This being the case we agreed Matt should spend the day there to see how he got on. At the end of that day I went to pick Matt up and have a de-briefing with Mr McCrone. He was still clearly unconvinced as to Matt's suitability to become a pupil of the Colne School. He told me at the de-briefing, "I couldn't understand a single word Matt spoke". Quick as a flash came the oh so clear retort from Matt, "Well I couldn't understand a word you said in Maths either!"

Despite Mr McCrone being a Chelsea supporter they became firm friends from that moment on. So it began, the Colne agreed to take Matt and now all we had to do was solve all the practical problems this would entail and there would be many! Two welfare assistants were appointed, their job description was basically to act as Matt's hands. These two ladies: Derryn and Carole, were worth their weight in gold going above and beyond their duties to ensure Matt's school life ran smoothly.

To avoid lifting either Matt or his chair we wanted, as far as possible, most of Matt's lessons to be on the ground floor. As you can imagine this was not only a timetable nightmare for the staff but for some subjects totally impractical. We had to adopt a "try it and see" policy. Most problems were overcome by the willingness of Derryn and Carole to help and their very positive and flexible attitudes.

Certain procedures needed to be addressed for the Fire authorities. For example, in the event of a fire they would need to know exactly where Matt was in the building at all times. Transport; getting Matt to and from school each day had to be arranged. Children from the surrounding area made the journey to school by double-decker bus, but this was not a viable option for Matt.

The local Education Authority agreed to fund a taxi to take Matt to and from school. This meant that every morning Barry or I would get Matt into the taxi with his bags and wheelchair and then, once at school, he was met by one of his welfare assistants who helped him out of the car and into his chair. The same was applied in reverse for the journey home.

Once Matt's timetable was in place Jan Compton came to the school to discuss with the site manager what adaptations would be required to meet Matt's needs. We walked around the premises together and identified where ramps would be useful. Matt also needed suitable toilet facilities, and the site manager made very convenient conveniences for him!

From the very beginning Barry and I made it totally clear that we were always available to help solve any problems that arose and would come into school at any time.

Matt's Head of Year, Mrs Jenny Versey, suggested we have termly meetings with Matt, Derryn, Carole and ourselves. This was a brilliant idea and enabled us to identify and deal with any problems and issues as they came along. As we had expected most problems were of a practical nature. One issue that arose was the need for an appropriate place to change for PE as both Matt's assistants were female. As previously mentioned Matt required suitable toilet facilities but the school is very large and so one site was not sufficient. Both problems were dealt with relatively easily, and having two toilets solved the changing for PE situation and the second toilet doubled up as a changing room.

On a more social level was Matt's difficulty to socialise with his peers at breaktimes. Being in a wheelchair meant he could only go where he was pushed and, lovely though his ladies were his friends didn't always want a grown up around. Jan's answer was an electric wheelchair that would allow him to follow his friends and also move around the school independently. Obviously the chair didn't happen overnight. First he had to be measured for it and after that we had to go over to Black Notley hospital so that Matt could take a driving test to prove he was safe to drive an electric chair.

When the chair finally arrived it made a huge difference to Matt's self esteem and independence around the school. He was enabled to carry his own books and whatever stuff he needed for the school day. I don't think he was always the best driver; some of the paintwork and furniture at the school bear a few scars.

A convenient space was made available to store the chair when not in use and also to charge the batteries overnight. Some teachers and students found it easier to accept Matt than others. Some of the staff were not enthusiastic to embrace the challenge of teaching an impaired student, others were very keen to make Matt a welcome and active participant in the lessons.

As parents we had to learn how to draw a very fine line between allowing Matt to be as normal a student as possible whilst ensuring he had the right level of support.

He must have done something right because he won an award for Effort and Attainment in his first year. All things considered Matt's first year had been successful and more importantly he had enjoyed school life. The Colne School also deserves credit for this.

COLNEHEAD

Matt's recollections:

Firstly, I must yet again thank everyone who helped me get to the Colne, a place where I had some good times and some bad times. Mr McCrone, I still don't understand what you were supposedly teaching us in maths! Deryn and Carole were my first two angels at the Colne and, although at times I got frustrated with their presence, I know I couldn't have done it without them, and we did have some right old laughs! Mum forgot to mention that after I got accepted to go to the Colne I was allowed to go one day a week before I started in the September. In all honesty, I got on better with the form I joined up with on that one day a week than I did with my eventual form. However, it meant I had more friends, and I'm not saying I didn't get on with people in my form because I did. The older children seem to accept me more easily which I think underlines the point I'm going to make below.

A lot of my mates from Alresford Primary School came to Colne with me, and at age eleven onwards, secondary school is all about image as the opposite sex is truly discovered. With this in mind, I was never going to be a gang leader, being accompanied by two middle-aged women is just not cool! A lot of the children would chat to me and we'd have a laugh but when it came to social events I was often excluded as it would mean me taking either Mum or Dad or having to rely on friends to help me, which at that age is asking too much, even when equipped with my chair. So my time at the Colne was a real eye opener and made me aware of my limitations and how children can be cruel. However, I do not bare any grudges as I was the first disabled student at the school and may have been the first some children had come across.

CHAPTER 30

ADOLESCENCE

Writing and reflecting on the ensuing years is difficult and at times painful. Adolescence is a challenging word to spell and even more so to deal with. The year 1992 brought home to roost how devastating emotionally and physically Matt's condition was, both for him and us as a family. Loneliness was the biggest problem. His only social activity spent with his peers was the weekly scout meeting.

Matt really enjoyed Scouts, the boys and the group leaders were very patient and he was generally accepted as just another member of the group. The leaders went the extra mile to make sure Matt could enjoy and participate in all their activities. But even they were seriously challenged when a weekend pot holing expedition in the Peak district came up. They asked if we could help. Well Barry suffers with claustrophobia so he was no use. No guesses as to who said they would give it a go! Alan had helped at scouts before but this was a huge ask. However he agreed. He was an expert at skiing down a mountain but this trip was the complete opposite. So on the Friday evening with great excitement and a certain amount of trepidation, they set off to the potholes and caves of the Peak district.

They arrived back home on Sunday night, absolutely exhausted but very proud of their achievements. Both of them had experienced blood curdling and heart stopping moments but as always came out smiling!

Sadly, apart from scouts, Matthew spent most of his time alone in his room either playing Nintendo or on his knees drawing. The muscles behind his knees and heels had tightened causing him to walk right up on his toes. This deterioration required surgery to lengthen the tendons behind his Achilles heel. The surgery meant he had to spend six weeks in plaster, and although it was successful it came at a price to his enjoyment and quality of life.

To explain, drawing was a large part of his relaxation and an outlet for some of life's frustrations. Finding a way to physically draw was an art in itself. Paper, pencils were laid on the floor for him. Matt knelt on the paper, gripping a pencil in his right hand. This could take several attempts. Once he had a firm grip on the pencil he wedged his hand between his knees using the inside of his thigh as a fulcrum. Some of the results were stunning, achieved through grim determination.

After the surgery Matt was told it would be unwise for him ever to kneel again, which was an enormous blow. We did try ways to overcome this, and even one of the Technology teachers at school took it on as a class project. The root of the problem was always Matt's involuntary movements, We could not find a way of keeping his trunk stable enough to allow his left arm to be held still; but his right arm have free movement. Eventually the frustration and failures proved too great and we had to accept a rare defeat.

We had completed some alterations to our home converting our dining room into a bedroom for Matt, and just across the hallway opposite to his room the downstairs loo had been adapted to provide suitable shower and toilet facilities for him.

From a practical point it made our lives a lot easier and gave Matt more independence but how I grew to hate that bedroom, especially the window. Matt's friends in the village were beginning to spread their wings and were gaining more independence. With the bus stop just up the road they could just hop on and go into Colchester or maybe into Brightlingsea or Clacton. They were riding their bikes further afield. All the things young people have every right to do as part of growing up and meeting life's new experiences. Matt could see their comings and goings through that window. In fairness Matt did go into Colchester on a few occasions but for him it couldn't ever be an impromptu action. The bus was impossible for him to manage, so if he was invited to join them on a trip into town we had to drive him and then once there assemble his scooter, after which we arranged where and when to pick him up.

Barry:

MATT RE-UNITES ME WITH UNITED

The Pony scooter had given Matt so much more independence and, on his regular Saturday trips into Colchester town centre, he invariably went into the Colchester United club shop. In the shop on most of these visits was John Schultz a former director of the club and a very long standing front man/host at the Colchester United ground and their club functions. Matt had told John about his Dad's playing days for Colchester. This was around about the time of my 40th birthday and lo and behold an invitation arrived for me to go as a guest of the club to Colchester's match with Rochdale which was taking place on my actual birthday. Also invited to the match were Wendy and Matt of course. This ended a period of twenty years since I last set foot in the ground, having always felt unhappy about how my career ended at the club. I've now been back involved with the club since that night and John Schultz has become a very good friend over that time.

There was however one occasion just before our "china" wedding anniversary when Matt went into

Colchester with two friends. We hadn't thought too much about it until the morning of our anniversary, when Matt presented us with two beautiful Royal Albert tea plates, a gift from him and Nikki. We were very pleased, but surprised and curious as to how Matt had managed to get the gift. The story gradually unfolded.

There is a large independent department store in Colchester and they happen to have a very fine and expensive china department. Matt had gone in on his scooter and was looking round the beautiful displays. As Matt was describing this to us our first thought was "Oh no, there's a large bill on its way!" We were wrong; it transpires that, as Matt went into the shop, he was very quickly met by two lady assistants. They came to Matt's aid and offered to fetch him anything at all he wanted to consider buying provided that he stayed in the one spot! Barry and I were helpless with laughter at this scenario, and Matt was delighted with himself and his purchases!

These outings stopped as Matt's dependence on his friends became too great a burden! Matt will continue:

Matt:

SHATTERING

I really enjoyed Scouts and had four fun years after finishing Cubs. Before I speak about Scouts, I need to let you into a funny story at Cubs. I had a friend, Luke Terry, who I used to have sleepovers with and we were called the troublesome twosome. One day we were drawing cartoon characters and we created our own: Quackergoose! For a good four years, Quackergoose did everything and was a large part of mine and Luke's friendship. Now, we were called the troublesome twosome because we knew how to make each other crack up in fits of laughter which often resulted in us both landing on the floor in hysterics. More often than not this was the position our mums found us in at the end of Cubs! Sorry Akela!

Another occasion when we got the fit of the giggles was on a train coming back from London after Mum and Dad took me and Luke there for my birthday. Luke noticed a man across the gangway from us who had fallen asleep, his eyes firmly over his belly and with the motion of the train, his head was constantly nodding. Well, we both completely lost it and I actually thought I was going to die as I could not catch breath especially as my parents were trying to tell us off whilst they themselves were laughing at us two! Fortunately I caught my breath an hour later.

As I said I had loads of great times at Scouts. Some of the highlights involved playing manhunt in the nearby woods, which if I may say so myself, I was good at because I was used to crawling on my knees and getting dirty so doing it in woods was no different. That was, until one night when we were playing manhunt in a nearby Scout camp which had a fairly big wood, so was perfect. We were all making our way back to the base trying to not get spotted, when all of a sudden about eight police vehicles with sirens blaring came and let's just say it wasn't only mud which Mum had to get out of my trousers! Well, the police were using those speakers to call us back to base urgently. It turns out we were part of a real manhunt as a mentally ill man had escaped from a local mental hospital and wasn't to be messed with!

As Mum mentioned, I went to the Peak District with the Scouts on an activity weekend, with my ever reliable uncle Alan. Such activities included abseiling, climbing and orienteering, all of which I had to try but apart from orienteering had little success. I was at the stage in my life when I was really frustrated by my limitations and so when I was pretty much lowered down the abseiling wall in a stretcher and was congratulated at the bottom for abseiling I got upset, as for me, that was not abseiling.

Whilst I was being upset over my 'abseiling exploits', a guy came over and said something along the lines of 'Hey, I see you crawl a lot, have you ever been pot holing before'? To which I nervously replied 'No' as I didn't have a clue what it was. The guy, who was frustrated at seeing my frustration, approached Alan and John Buckner, my Scout Leader, and asked them if it would be ok to take me pot holing, obviously with Alan in tow, to which they agreed.

Well, it seems, I was born thirty years too late as I would have made a good cave explorer! We were lowered twenty metres underground, armed with waterproofs and helmets, with head torches, and told to keep up with the guy. The caves had to be tackled by crawling which as you can imagine suited me but not quite so Alan. We crawled for about 45 minutes through pools of water and saw thousands of stalagmites and stalactites, I was in my element, although cold. At the end of the *crawlathon* the cave opened up and there was a crystal clear, 20 feet deep pond, it was truly amazing. We spent about ten minutes admiring it before the guy said we had 90 minutes in which to crawl back before the cave fills with ice cold water! (So much for health and safety!) Anyway, we made it out alive, both mine and Alan's faces aglow with happiness and exhaustion. We met up with the other Scouts and made them sick with jealousy, a strange but great feeling!

Drawing was a major part of my life as Mum has already mentioned. I took great satisfaction copying pictures of airplanes from a book and I must say I had Spitfires to a tee! As well as drawing planes I loved to take myself to a burnt out old church, situated not far from our house, and sit for hours drawing what I saw! This to me was my way of relaxing, and I had more cause to draw once Nikki was around as she loved her Disney characters, so of course, being big Bro I had to draw for her bedroom wall and my best ever drawing was of Mickey Mouse, which I believe/hope Mum still has. So when I was told I could not draw how I always used to it came as a real blow to me, especially as I was due to take it as one of my chosen GCSE subjects and one which I was confident of getting a good grade for I had achieved a B in the mock.

However much you constantly try new ways to tackle a problem, there comes a point where trying becomes more of a hindrance, as was the case with me trying to draw. No blame goes to Mum and Dad as my stubborn streak wouldn't let me admit defeat and I became more frustrated, and that frustration impacted on my concentration on other subjects as, not only could I not draw, I couldn't write anymore so had to rely on my carers to do it for me. Meanwhile I was daydreaming and not paying attention. I've since realized that shit does happen and there are things that, although it's hard, we must accept are out of our reach, no matter how hard we try.

BARRY:

One door closes and another opens! Life wasn't always a drudge.We did discover another thing that Matt could do! And that was drive a go-kart.

We had brilliant family holidays and we socialised with family and friends at numerous functions, parties and barbeques. Matt and Nik plus parents had great fun go-karting in real go-karts at Jean and Roger's. Very much off-roading as part of the circuit went through trees in Jean and Roger's wood!! Again this was something that Matt "could do"!

CHAPTER 31

FISHING

Finding ways of getting Matt out of his room and involved in a hobby he could really enjoy became a mission for all of us. As Nikki has previously said it was this isolation that made her realize that Matt's disabilities really made him "different" from others, but also brought the two of them even closer. Barry had always enjoyed fishing and so he took Matt one day and he was hooked! They joined the local Angling club and Barry had a telescopic pole made for Matt. So now on most Saturday mornings, accompanied by Alan, they headed off to the club waters.

One of the lakes was especially accessible enabling Barry to park almost at the water's edge. Barry and Alan took it in turns to sit beside Matt, baiting the hook and casting out. Matt learnt to strike independently by tucking the pole under his armpit. If the strike was successful Matt played the fish whilst Barry or Alan got ready with the landing net. To this day Matt is still a keen fisherman and, whenever he gets the opportunity and a willing helper, spends hours trying to catch the big one!

There is another little anecdote coming here, written by Barry as he was the featured hero! On one Saturday morning session during late summer early autumn Barry's dedication was tested to the maximum.

Matt had not been a fisherman for long as he was still using his 10ft custom built whip. This particular day saw them all catching fish quite successfully when suddenly Matt's float shot under the water!!

Was it a great bite from a big fish? Just as quickly his rod disappeared from the rests and into the lake before either Alan or Barry could grab it. Matt burst into floods of tears for two reasons:

1.   The loss of his rod

2.   The loss of a rather large fish!!

Barry's words continue the tale:

> *The lake is quite large, probably the size of two football pitches and to see Matt's bright green rod ploughing up, down and across the lake at some considerable speed (it floats by the way) was quite funny!*
>
> *Matt however failed to see the comedy, and Barry had the bright idea to strip down to his underpants, and go into the lake to retrieve the speeding rod. He swam some 50yards out to the middle of the lake, treading water as it's about 12 feet deep there. He can hear Matt's sobs quietening in anticipation of the unfolding drama. Barry manages to intercept the torpedo rod and the fish is still hooked and fighting. With great skill (Barry's words) he manages to play the fish whilst still treading water. Matt is now shrieking with delight at the prospect of both fish and rod being returned to shore.*
>
> *Gradually Barry is winning the battle to get back with the fighting fish still in tow. Matt is by now falling about with laughter as Barry reaches the shallow margins of the lake. The water there is only chest deep when suddenly the fish makes one final lunge for freedom and "bang", the line snaps, and the fish (almost definitely a carp) is gone to fight another day. As a weed covered muddy man in soggy underpants emerges from the water he hears Matt's howls of frustration once again because his dad has lost the fish!*

For all future fishing expeditions Matt's rods were anchored to a bank stick with a length of very strong elastic! Although fishing provided some respite from his loneliness it could not compensate for the teenage life he had been robbed of. Occasionally school friends came round and played on the Playstation or Nintendo with him, but as soon as a better offer came along they disappeared. This is not in any way a criticism of the youngsters, just telling it as it was. If it was difficult for us to handle, we can only imagine how painful and frustrating it was for Matt.

The school holidays were the worst, especially the long summer break. When out walking the dogs with Barry I would cry endlessly and question and doubt our determination to ensure Matt had as normal life as possible. By doggedly fighting the route we had taken, were our efforts now condemning Matt to a life of feeling second class? Matt was consistently struggling and striving harder than his peers just to be accepted. I vividly remember one occasion when he remarked life was bad enough if your trainers weren't the right label, so what chance did you have when your body didn't work properly!

There is only one person who can answer my question and I'm sure his reply changes frequently.

Matt:

CONFORMING IS BORING

So Matt believes!!

In reply to my remark many moons ago I have this to say; conforming is boring! As I've said in an earlier chapter, secondary school is all about image and trainers were just one example. Like the old adage goes 'with age comes wisdom', this is very true. For most of my life I spent every effort trying to fit in and it has caused not only myself but my family a great deal of angst and heartbreak, but it has only been within the last few years that I've learnt that I didn't need other

150

people to accept me, I needed to accept myself! It may sound really deep, and I'm not going to deny that, but it is something we must all do before we can be happy. I could go on about this for many pages but I shall save that for my book!

It is true what Mum said, I did feel isolated and was constantly trying to be accepted when I was young, but it must be said I did not and do not blame anyone for it, especially not my parents as I hope my comments in this book make very clear. Having said that though, I will not forgive Dad for letting that whopping fish go! For me, going fishing with Dad and Alan meant the world to me and I have some fantastic memories. Although Dad jumping in after my pole is a standout. Fishing was and still is a passion of mine and has contributed to my competitive streak as fishing trips with Dad always became a competition and more often than not I would come out victor! You know it's true Dad hahaha!

CHAPTER 32

HEAD POINTER

School life presented new challenges. After the surgery on his heel any independence he had with art etc. was extinct and so we had to explore alternatives. As I have previously mentioned a technology teacher made it her mission to try and come up with an alternative, but every idea she had proved beyond Matt's poor hand control and was at the mercy of his involuntary movements.

ICT seemed to be the way forward and so Matt was visited and assessed by the Local Education Authority's ICT advisor. She recommended a word processor with a head pointer to operate it.

Initially Matt felt very self-conscious and who wouldn't with a stick protruding from your forehead! He was also worried he could take someone's eye out as he turned his head. But in his usual determined manner he persisted and found his own way round the problem, becoming proficient with both and this is how he managed it. As we said the stick protruding from Matt's forehead was potentially lethal and so Matt told us to take the stick off. He used the ball to which the stick was connected to type with.

The constant problem Matt had was of dribbling, now a real embarrassment to him. It was also a problem to the keyboard. A rubber sleeve, similar to those used on supermarket tills, was the answer. The sleeve went over the keyboard keeping the keys protected and dry. He can still type very well in this manner but again it comes at a price, in that Matt suffers with a great deal of pain in the neck. A legacy of typing in this fashion for all these years, mind you he has neck muscles that any body builder would be proud of! Matt continues:

Matt:

SWALLOW, NOT SPIT!

As Mum has mentioned throughout this book, I have always had issues with dribbling (and not just a football!) and often get told off by Mum. I dribble when I'm tired, concentrating on something or when I'm relaxed, so you guessed it, pretty much all the time. I know it's not attractive and whilst out in public I do make a concerted effort not to dribble. When I was getting used to my head pointer I had to concentrate on keeping my head quite still in order to tap on the correct buttons. This was made more problematic due to the stick being about 30 centimetres long. As Mum said I was lethal with my head pointer. I felt like a Dalek and every time I lifted my head I would endanger anyone who sat in close proximity. Then I just used the ball to type with until I went to university and typing became more intense and played havoc with my neck. So one day a friend suggested I shorten the metal stick with a jig saw to about six centimeters. Now, I'm typing this with the same six centimeter stick and touch wood my neck is okay but not great.

CHAPTER 33

DOGS

Not all of 1992/93 was depressing there were also many good times.

Losing our dog Sugar in January left a large hole in our lives that we needed to fill. Shirley tried to persuade me to get the children a puppy. I didn't feel I had the time or energy to train a puppy, so I very glibly told her the only puppy I would consider was an issue of her brother Charlie's black Labrador; Tess. Tess was often having "phantom pregnancies" but at seven years old she was unlikely to ever have pups!

In the February half term we visited the Wood Green Animal shelter in Huntingdon to see if there was a suitable pet for us. Living where we did was and still is a perfect place for dogs. At Wood Green we peered into kennel after kennel of beseeching eyes and wagging tails until we spotted a border collie that looked a likely candidate. We went back to the reception desk to organise a walk with him. Unfortunately another family had beaten us to it. The lady on the desk took pity on our crestfallen faces, and breaking all the rules told us about a stray lurcher that had just been brought into the shelter. The dog hadn't had any assessments done, but she felt he might just be what we were looking for and so she brought him out to meet us.

They had named him Freddie and thought he was about a year old.

Sporting a very tatty orange woolly coat Freddie marched straight over to Matt, sat down in front of him, looked him in the eye and then laid his head on Matt's lap. Fait Accompli! Both children were instantly smitten; but as Freddie had just come into the shelter it would be eight days before his assessments were completed. If, after that time, he was considered suitable we could make the long trip back and rescue him!

Eight days later the shelter rang and told us they were confident he would make a lovely pet. He was most importantly, good natured and gentle around children. The downside was that he was extremely thin and was suffering with sarcoptic mange. We were advised that what Freddie needed most was lots of TLC! We agreed to pick him up the following day. Very late that same night we had another phone call, this time from Shirley. Tess's latest phantom pregnancy had produced 3 black and 2 yellow puppies! They believed the culprit father was the golden retriever from the neighbouring farm. Charlie, Shirley's brother said we could have first pick of the litter!

The next day was very cold and snowing hard. We picked Grandma up and made the seventy mile journey to Huntingdon. We arrived at the shelter and saw Freddie minus his woolly coat. The coat had concealed the severity of his emaciation and skin complaint.

Barry was not convinced that taking Freddie on was one of our better ideas and I was inclined to agree with him. We didn't stand a chance. With Grandma on their side the children and Freddie's pleas won the day. We replaced the woolly coat with a very stylish Barbour jacket and brought him home.

The treatment for the mange was cold washes in foul smelling shampoo which had to dry on. It was February and freezing but this dog allowed us to subject him to this indignity with implicit trust in his eyes. We gave him a lovely warm bed and buckets of the prescribed TLC. The children had adored him on sight and clearly Freddie thought he had died and gone to doggy heaven! The skin treatment worked and soon revealed a beautiful glossy coat.

What about Tess's puppy?   We went to visit Charlie a couple of days later and instantly fell for the larger yellow puppy. She was adorable and we were a lost cause. We named her Bonnie and brought her home seven weeks later on my 40th birthday.   But how would Freddie react? Given that during the short time we had had him he would chase anything and we couldn't let him off the lead!   Our concerns were groundless. Just when he thought life couldn't get any better we gave him the best present in the world. It was love at first sight and the start of a truly wonderful, happy and extremely entertaining partnership. Bonnie and Freddie were inseparable, a real double act that gave us years of faithful pleasure. True partners in crime, happiest most when outside in the garden playing with Matt and Nikki!

As I write this chapter in October 2007 Bonnie has sadly died but Freddie is still with us at the grand old age of 16 plus, still ruling the roost and still the apple of the children's eye. Barry and I are also firmly convinced that rescuing Freddie was a good idea!

Matt:

A DOG'S TALE

Following on from our losses in that year I truly believe Fred was destined to belong to us and I think Nikki's, Grandma's and my decision to make it so was one of the best decisions we ever made. It has been a joke since we got him that Dad never liked him. However, truthfully Dad has grown to adore him. Getting Bonnie was wonderful, although at first it was with great anxiousness and trepidation as we were petrified to see how Freddie reacted and, oh my goodness, I don't think I've ever seen anything so incredible! We truthfully believed Fred would see Bonnie as a rabbit that he could chew or get jealous of her stealing his new found kingdom. Then our nerves were really shot when Bonnie made a beeline for Fred's bed whilst he was looking at her oddly. Before I continue, I must explain Fred's bed was his sanctuary, his most prized possession and definitely his. So with baited breath and feelings of helplessness we watched Bonnie invade Fred's Mecca! To our astonishment, Fred welcomed her in and about thirty minutes later was a fully-fledged male mummy dog. He would put his head over her head when he decided it was her bedtime.

One of the most memorable and loveliest memories I have of Freddie and Bonnie is when she was very little and was no taller than the Daffodils in our garden. It was raining and, as Fred walked up the garden path, Bonnie was walking underneath him so she wouldn't get wet.

CHAPTER 34

MEETING RYAN GIGGS

Matt loves most sport especially football and he is an ardent Manchester United fan.

In 1992 our niece Claire had a boyfriend who happened to be a friend of the Norwich City's reserve goalkeeper, Mark Walton. To cut a long story to the bone Mark very kindly got four tickets for Norwich's home tie against Manchester United and not only that, he got passes for the player's lounge. The excitement in our household was tangible! Just before Barry, Matt, Claire and her boyfriend headed off to Carrow Road for the match I asked Matt what he would say if he got to meet his idol Ryan Giggs. Feeling total disbelief that this might be a possibility he couldn't answer me.

Their seats were in the Norwich supporters' stand, and Matt took a lot of good-natured ribbing because he was supporting the opposition!

After the match, which Manchester United won 3-1 Matt and company went into the very crowded players' lounge. Barry parked Matt in his wheelchair by the door and headed off, armed with Matt's autograph book. Both sets of player's cheerfully signed Matthew's book. Barry then came across Ryan Giggs enjoying a quiet drink; he also signed Matt's book, then plucking up courage Barry asked Ryan if he would come and say hello to Matthew. Ryan agreed and told Barry to lead the way.

Now you need to picture the scene. The lounge was a very crowded room, Matt sitting in his chair taking it all in but not able to see above heads. Barry is quite tall just shy of 6 foot, Ryan Giggs is smaller and shorter. Matt spots his dad coming towards him wearing a huge grin and saying "Guess who has come to say hello to you?" Barry steps aside to reveal Ryan Giggs! Matt was rendered unusually speechless. Ryan chatted to him for a few minutes about the match and then posed for a photo.

What pressure on poor Claire to make sure it was a good one! The photo now framed is still one of his most prized possessions and the envy of some of his friends.

BARRY:

Once Matt turned ten, football really was his main interest. He started to play fantasy football in a league; and soon his knowledge of the then current Premier League players was far greater than mine. We also went to quite a few major matches with the biggest moment being the Norwich Man U match that Wendy has described previously.

Matt also witnessed the Eric Cantona drama at Crystal Palace when he "attacked" a fan and ended up with a prolonged suspension from the game. Matt and I both agree, having witnessed the event and seen the evidence and reports, that the fan got what he deserved.

We also saw Colchester United play in all three of their Wembley matches to date, and, in addition to this, a Championship playoff final between Crystal Palace and Sheffield United at the same venue which was a hugely enjoyable experience for us all.

Later on that year we took the children up to Old Trafford. Unfortunately we were unable to get on an official tour of the stadium but one of the stewards allowed us into the Trophy room and museum and then sneaked us into the stadium. The Holy Grail!

Just before we met this very kind steward Barry and Matt in his wheelchair were waiting outside the club shop when a large black car pulled up alongside them, down went the passenger window and a very Scottish voice and familiar head asked Matt if he was having a good time! It was of course Sir Alex who then chatted to Matt for a few seconds, and then after he was driven off we were approached by the steward.

CHAPTER 35

DISNEYWORLD

In the summer of 1993 we booked a holiday to Florida. Both Matt and Nikki were very keen to experience a "Disney" holiday and so were we. We had also arranged to meet up with the Baxters as they were going to be in Florida about the same time.

All was going very well on our outward flight until we hit a thunderstorm. It was just like being on a giant roller coaster. I am not the most confident of air travellers so this experience was really scary. We were not allowed out of our seats and even the cabin crew were only taking off their belts for emergencies! The pilot then informed us that the control tower in Orlando had been struck by lightning so we would have to make an emergency landing in Tampa! How much worse could it get? Once "safely" landed in Tampa we sat in the plane on the tarmac and through the window watched the storm raging. The palm trees were being blown horizontal and the plane was rocking from side to side.

After about an hour the pilot told us we would be taking off again as soon as he could get a slot. Matt and I were so frightened we would gladly have walked the eighty miles to Orlando! We eventually landed there late but in one piece after our white-knuckle experience.

Once through Customs etc. we went to pick up the hire car. We had been given a good map so Barry was confident it wouldn't be long before we got to the hotel and bed. Unfortunately the storms had swung the overhead signs around rendering the map useless!

One of the reasons I married Barry was for his extraordinary sense of direction and I am so glad I did. We finally reached our hotel at 5.00am.

Both children had been brilliant during the journey and I remember, once we got to our hotel and bedroom, I just pointed Nikki in the direction of her bed and she was asleep before her head hit the pillow!

Cheryl had been phoning the hotel and was obviously worried when we hadn't arrived, but later that day calm was restored all round and Cheryl and I spoke on the phone, arranging to meet them at Universal Studios in two days time.

Nikki's six-year old face seeing Disneyworld for the first time was absolutely magical and for us all looking up Mainstreet to Sleeping Beauty's Castle was a very emotional and magical experience though it sounds cheesy. Matt thoroughly enjoyed it too. Getting around in his wheelchair was made so easy; there were ramps and alternative exits and entrances wherever necessary. All the parks are fabulous but it was extremely tiring trying to see as much as possible, you need to arrive early and stay as late as your stamina will allow.

To take our feet off the gas for a while we decided to have a look around Oldtown in Kissimee, and strolling along the sidewalks we came across Grimm's haunted house. The "Ghoul" and the "Vampire" characters patrolling outside persuaded us to enter. I wasn't too sure but Matt and even little Nikki were both keen to go in. The billboards advertised that "live" actors were inside but we were told if we didn't touch them they wouldn't touch us! So in we went, leaving Matt's wheelchair at the entrance.

It was very spooky; Barry was holding Matt up to walk, with Nikki and I bringing up the rear. Yeah, the actors didn't touch us but they did jump out and give chase. And of course being the only people in there we got their undivided attention! It occurred to Barry and me that absolutely nobody else in the world knew we were there so if the Smiths were never seen again! Matt thought it was brilliant but pointed out afterwards that he

162

had been the one pushed out in front with the rest of us cowering behind him!

The whole holiday was great but Matt being Matt had to ensure he got more than his fair share of attention and sitting around the hotel pool one day he put another of his plans into action, he "accidently" fell into the pool and then thought it hilarious when Barry dived in to "save" him. The joke however backfired on him when he tried the stunt a second time and ignored by us. He was hauled out by a complete stranger who had jumped in fully clothed. The little boy who had cried "wolf" was very firmly put in his place!

We finished our holiday with a leisurely week in Clearwater, enjoying the beach and playing lots of mini golf. A fantastic time was had by all.

CHAPTER 36

SHORT OF FINANCE

Matt was now into his second and third years at Secondary school and GCSE 0 levels were not a million miles away. He was considered to be a bright student so it was essential that we, along with the school, got organized to prepare for these all-important exams.

The Exam boards were notified of Matt's special needs to allow them to consider any extra assistance he could be entitled to.

We arranged a visit to the Wolfson Centre which is part of Gt Ormond Street Hospital. At the centre they specialise in assessing children with special needs for IT and communication aids. One of the teachers from the Colne came with us.

As you know Matt had a computer at home which he operated with his head pointer. As I have explained this worked very well but, if he used it for prolonged periods, it did cause him to suffer with stiff neck and headaches.

After some discussion and practical assessment the Wolfson team came up with a computer system operated by switches attached to the headrest on his electric chair.

Obviously this system would alleviate the RSI (repetitive stress injury) to his neck which in turn would hopefully reduce the number of headaches he suffered.

The programme, called "Headmaster" cost £1500, and the designer agreed to come into the school and give a demonstration. If it looked suitable Matt could try it out for two weeks free of charge. At the demonstration the head of the school's IT department promised to make a Windows 3.1 computer available to Matt for the two weeks. We were confident this system was the answer to

Matt's neck problems. The local Rotary club had shown an interest in helping with cost.

Matt came home from school a few days later, absolutely crestfallen. Despite promises to the contrary the school had said they couldn't spare a computer for Matt to use for two weeks, so he was unable to give the programme a fair go. I was so angry. It was so frustrating and bitterly disappointing. Barry and I now fully realised that the technology was out there to help our son but it was beyond our financial means.

As I have mentioned earlier we had often been asked why we hadn't pursued a claim for compensation on Matt's behalf.

Our argument had always been that no amount of money could change how Matt was and that we could provide for all his needs.

Those beliefs were now proven naïve and unrealistic. Computer technology was the way forward, not just for the short term, but to help for the rest of his life. Our new way of thinking also encompassed our own vulnerability. At present we were young and healthy but what would happen if that should change? Matt was going to need care and support for the rest of his life, which was almost certainly going to be beyond our lifetime.

Some years before Barry had been given the card of a solicitor in Cambridge who specialised in medical litigation. For reasons unknown he had kept the card and now digging it out of his wallet he made a phone call.

The call lasted a very long time. Robert Longhurst was the name of the solicitor and, after listening to Barry, he invited us to meet him in his Cambridge office. Never having much experience of solicitors before we went along, very unsure of what to expect but confident it was the right thing to do.

After listening very carefully to our story surrounding Matt's birth and the ensuing years Mr Longhurst told us he had a real gut feeling that we had a good case. He cautioned us that in his experience it was going to be a long and hard road ahead. He likened it to a steeplechase; after you cleared one hurdle another was just around the bend.

The first hurdle was to get a Legal Aid certificate enabling the solicitors to look at the medical records.

The first task for Barry and me, was to individually write a statement leading up to and immediately after Matt's birth. We went home a little dazed at the possible magnitude of the task we were taking on.

Writing our individual statements we found a difficult and painful exercise, but after we had finished and compared them we were amazed at their clarity and how almost identical our individual memories were.

It was as Barry described like an exorcism. Those deeply buried thoughts and memories were brought out and committed to paper.

We had made the first advance into an eight year legal battle we were prepared to fight on behalf of our son.

BARRY:

As Wendy describes we began the legal action in 1993 whilst I was still very much working for the Prudential. This was at a time when, for the 10,000 plus field staff, an absolute mega change was in process! Restructuring—Reorganising—Re-applying for my position/role.

Gone were the days of good old "Auntie Pru." Till now as long as I worked as best I could they had been very supportive about such things as time off for Matt's appointments etc. Under the newly arriving regime, if you weren't either out in the field (with clients) or in the office you were a NEG (negative worker). This all happened to coincide with the increased need for Wendy and me to attend meetings, assessments in connection with both Matt's medical and educational needs but also the court action which got more and more intense the further along the litigation road we travelled.

CHAPTER 37

A DYNAMIC GEORDIE

We were very sorry to lose Derryn as one of Matt's assistants, but sadly she hurt her back in an accident and was unable to continue in her role. Derryn was replaced for a time by a lady called Maggie, she was also great with Matt but eventually Maggie left for pastures new.

Enter now a diminutive, dynamic Geordie called Gill. Matt, Carole and Gill made an excellent team and became firm friends. Like Nikki, Gill fulfilled many roles in Matt's life, including senior advisor and Agony aunt. From a parent's point of view it was reassuring to know Matt had someone he could really talk to and confide in. Gill never revealed a single confidence but on occasions was able to alert us to a problem. Gill took notes for Matt during lessons and also photo copied worksheets from text books.

Using his word processor and head pointer worked well for recording his work. Revising for exams was however proving to be a problem. Matt couldn't select or turn the pages of a book independently and accurately. I hit upon the idea of reading his textbooks onto cassette tapes. Matt was able to operate his cassette player once a tape had been loaded for him. For the following years my voice droned on through many a subject. I felt so sorry for him having to listen to it over and over again.

To most teenagers listening to their mum's voice going on and on is purgatory and Matt is no exception but he was a captive audience! But as his exam results proved my idea worked!

I have to include a little anecdote here purely because it is my comeback whenever he trots out the "You've never liked me" story.

Drama was one of Matt's favourite subjects and on one occasion he became so enthusiastic that he fell off a table and knocked himself out. It was in the days before mobile phones and "sod's law" both Barry and I (unusually) were out. Unable to contact us, the school phoned for an ambulance and Matt, escorted by Carole, was a blue light job to casualty.

Eventually Barry and I were contacted and went straight to the hospital. The doctor told us that Matt was fine, but just as a precaution they were doing half hourly observations after which he could go home very soon. I was taken to the cubicle where Matt was lying, attached to an automatic pulse and blood pressure machine.

He looked very pale and dramatic and burst into tears when he saw me. I hugged him, told him he was fine and that he hadn't done any damage. I assured him the doctors were so pleased with him he could come home soon.

Taking great gulps of air and waving at the machine he was attached to he wailed; "So why am I on a Life Support machine?"

An Oscar winning performance!

CHAPTER 38

SKIING

Every year the Colne School organised a ski trip, Matthew was very keen to have a go but unfortunately this was not a viable option. One day whilst watching Newsround on television there was a feature about the Uphill Ski Club. The club was founded by a group of expert skiers, who after a day on the slopes were reflecting on how exhilarating it was to ski down a mountain. Their thoughts turned to people with disabilities and how ski equipment could be adapted so that anybody and everybody could enjoy this experience. The Uphill Ski Club was born.

Alan is a keen and competent skier and when we told him about the club he suggested we find out more and so the four of us went along to the club's next AGM. During the meeting we met lots of skiers and would-be skiers with all manner of disabilities. Some were experienced and some like Matt keen to try.

The club explained how the trips were organised. Each skier was teamed with a "Buddy". A buddy could be a competent skier or a willing volunteer offering physical and practical support.

Alan booked himself onto the "buddie's" course being held the following weekend. He enjoyed the course and agreed to accompany Matt on the club's next trip to Schladming in Austria.

We had never considered skiing to be a possibility for Matt but with the aid of the adaptive equipment available he eventually became a keen and competent skier. How?

Obviously Matt couldn't hold ski poles so a "ski bra" was attached to his skis keeping them straight and parallel. Matt anchored his hands between his knees to prevent the involuntary movements disrupting his balance. The rest was practice, practice and more practice and of course lots of tumbles!

Can you imagine the anxiety and anticipation we felt at their first homecoming? We were so desperate to hear all about it. Barry and I arranged to meet them from the coach at the Services near to Dover. Their coach finally arrived; we were so excited and immediately went over to the coach to help them off. Barry went to retrieve their suitcases and I went to help Matt down the steps. The squeal that greeted me as I grabbed Matt's hand was piercing! Mum had done it again, for, unbeknown to me; Matt had dislocated his thumb whilst ski-ing and I had just grabbed the offended appendage!

Watching Alan's video and seeing Matt and all the other skiers whizzing down the slopes was amazing. It made us feel proud and very humbled by their achievements. The "Apres ski" had also been an overwhelming success and a very popular experience!

Personal pride in their triumph was priceless and shared by all the "buddies." The tales they recounted kept us entertained for hours. Hopefully one day Matt will write his own story and we shall learn even more.

Matt and Alan went on the next five annual trips with the USC, the last one being to Boston in 1998. Unfortunately by the time of this last trip Matt's hip was so bad it could no longer bear his weight and so he had to come down the mountain in a bi-ski, which Matt said just wasn't the same as feeling the snow under your feet.

CHAPTER 39

THE LEGAL BATTLE INTENSIFIES

Our quest for compensation for Matt was moving along very slowly. The application for a Legal Aid certificate enabling us to see copies of the medical records surrounding Matt's birth was initially turned down, par for the course apparently. Our solicitors appealed and the decision was reversed.

The copies of the medical records were finally received by our solicitor and, although they were of poor quality and two important records were missing, it meant we could now engage a Consultant Obstetrician and a Consultant Paediatrician to look at them.

I should explain here that when a case of medical negligence is made the claimant has to prove that negligence has occurred. Expert witnesses are engaged by the legal team to prepare an individual and unbiased report, giving their opinions on how and why the injuries were sustained. It also involves forecasting how those injuries will affect the rest of the victim's life. If a case goes to court these expert witnesses can be called to testify and their reports used as evidence. Obviously the opposing side, in our case the Health Authority, would engage their own expert witnesses.

It sounds quite straightforward on paper but of course my "summing up" of the situation is very basic and simplistic. The reality is far more complicated. In December 1996 we had to travel to Leeds, where Matt was examined and we were interviewed by a Consultant Paediatrician engaged by our solicitor to be an expert witness. He recommended that Matt should have an MRI scan to rule out any congenital defect and to prove conclusively the birth episode was the cause of his brain damage.

172

The MRI scan took place at the London Independent Hospital on 27th June 1997. The nurses looking after Matt told him there was something very "football" about his room for apparently the previous occupant had been Jamie Redknapp! The MRI revealed that Matt's brain damage was in no way congenital, but had been caused by trauma occurring around his birth. This all-important information meant we were still in the steeplechase.

1st September 1997 was the date of our appointment to see a Harley Street Obstetrician. His main interest was my pregnancy and the progression of my labour. He went over my labour almost minute by minute making demands on my memory for times and details. At the end of the interview he made it clear that without the foetal heart trace and the partogram (which were the two missing records) it was going to be very hard for him to make a report strong enough to support a claim of negligence. If we could produce these all important records the situation would be very different.

I felt crestfallen, it was the day after Princess Diana had died and our mood matched London's very sombre one, as we walked back to Liverpool St Station via Leicester Square and Covent Garden. I need to explain what the two missing records were and why they were so vital.

1. The foetal heart traces were produced by the CTG machine, which is the monitoring device for the baby's foetal heart rate. (This was the device we were told during my labour had been misbehaving).
2. The partogram is the document on which the progress of labour is plotted.

What followed over the next months cemented a solid foundation for our claim. The initial copies of the records provided by the Health Authority were on microfilm and, as I have said, were of very poor quality. In November 1997 Mr Longhursts' associate, Mr Paul Taylor, visited the hospital to look at the original microfilm records. He thought by looking at the original microfiche he might get a clearer image. He discovered the copies provided to us were incomplete and also it appeared the hospital might well have kept the missing CTG but in a different place. Improved copies of the records and the CTG were requested from the Health Authority but neither were forthcoming. This seemed extremely suspicious to us, but whether the missing CTG was intentionally misfiled or misplaced we shall never know.

In February 1998 our solicitors applied to the Court to obtain an Order requiring the Defendants to produce the CTG and microfilm records.

As a result of this order the improved copies of the records and a copy of the CTG were eventually received by our solicitors in May 1998. This revealing information was then passed on to our expert witnesses for examination. The Obstetrician and Paediatrician suggested we have an expert CTG technician look at and interpret the trace. Our Legal Aid certificate was amended to allow all of this to happen. A great deal of correspondence and debate took place between our solicitor and the three medical experts.

Finally in April 1999 we received a copy of the Paediatric report; it makes heartbreaking reading.

I quote from parts of it:
"The clinical evidence and the MRI report point undoubtedly to peri-natal asphyxia as the cause of Matthew's disabilities. It is extremely unlikely that if earlier intervention had occurred and Matthew had been born by 18.10hrs that he would have suffered the brain damage that he has done."

The report does not go into full obstetric details but describes what happened immediately before and after Matthew's birth.

"At around 7pm that evening the Obstetrician and Midwives noted that there were type 11 dips where the foetal heart rate dropped to 60 beats per minute and took 3 minutes to recover and it was decided to undertake an emergency Caesarean section.

"At 7.35pm an Anaethetist was informed, but was already in theatre at the County Hospital with an anaesthetised patient and was therefore unable to attend. There were then attempts to contact the Consultant Anaesthetist, but the Caesarean section did not take place for some time and Matthew was born at 20.15 hours.The operative notes clearly read that the indication for Caesarean section was severe foetal distress with a foetal heart at the start of the operation of 40 beats a minute."

"Taking Matthew's weight and head circumference it would appear that they are both on the 25th centile which shows that both his body and head were growing normally prior to delivery."

"There is, in other words, no evidence of intrauterine growth retardation. In the paediatric notes the placenta was described as being healthy and weighing 0.6grams. I assume this means 0.6kgs. There therefore appears to be no evidence of any problems with the placenta prior to birth, but again you will need to rely upon the obstetric expert."

"Matthew was extremely ill at birth. The only sign of life was a very slow heart rate. He was making no respiratory effort. He had no muscle tone. There were no reflex responses. He was pale. He was therefore given an Apgar score of 1. A baby in good condition would have an Apgar score of 10. The paediatric notes report that the umbilical cord was tightly round Matthew's neck (this would have been prior to delivery)

"Matthew required immediate resuscitation by the Paediatric team. An endotracheal tube was inserted and he was given intermittent positive pressure ventilation."

"At the age of 3 minutes Matthew was given Sodium Bicarbonate intravenously. A further dose was given at 5 minutes as was 25micrograms of Narcan. It would also appear from the paediatric notes he was also given 100 mgs of Narcan at 2 minutes".

"The Apgar score at 5 minutes was calculated as 4. By now his heart rate had returned to normal and he appeared to be making some respiratory effort. However he had no muscle tone, remained pale in colour and showed no reflexes. I believe there had been a miscalculation in the Apgar score and this should have been recorded as 3 at 5 minutes."

"By 10 minutes his heart rate continued to remain strong, again he was making little respiratory effort. He had no muscle tone, his colour had now improved in that he was blue rather than pale. And he was beginning to show some reflex response. This gave him an Apgar score of 5 at 10 minutes. He was reported to have taken his first gasp at 6 minutes, but did not begin regular respirations until he was 15 minutes old."

The notes go on to observe and record Matthew's condition during the following days, as I recalled earlier in the book.

It breaks my heart all over again not to be able to change any of it. With this report and also the reports from the obstetrician and CTG technician our solicitors wrote to the defendants' solicitors on the 10th May 1999 informing them of our evidence of medical negligence.

BARRY:

The miles of travelling required in connection with various assessments for the legal case took us to such exotic places as Leeds and Dewsbury to name just a couple. There were also several trips to London prior to Matt's surgery and obviously afterwards as well.

One really good thing amongst all this was that in December 1998 I left the Pru and went Independent. I was self employed and accountable to no one! Obviously I still had to earn a living and by virtue of no longer being tied to just one company and their product range found it no problem; and greatly improved both income and quality of life.

CHAPTER 40

ISOLATION

Of course whilst due process of our compensation claim was chugging along in the background our everyday lives continued. I am going to be backtracking now to 1994/95.

Matthew was academically doing reasonably well. His best subjects were History and, unbelievably, German! Everything was shaping into place for the not too distant 'O' Levels.

Still sadly lacking was a social life. Fishing continued to be his main hobby but other than that he rarely left his bedroom.

Reflecting on these times I agonise now, as I did then, as to whether I could have changed the situation in any way. I had even considered advertising.

WANTED

Teenage company for lonely boy
With cerebal palsy.

No, I still think I was right not to. Matt is very proud, and as all parents of teenagers know, embarrassment must be avoided at all costs. It would have ruined what little street cred he had, but at that time I was so desperately sorry for him. It was a period we just had to get through and hope for better times ahead. I would like to share with you a poem written by Matt and included in a book of poetry published by the Colne School.

LIFELINE

By Matthew Smith

The day I came out of my mummy's tum
No-one thought I'd live
Because I was dead.
Yes.
DEAD!
You might be wondering
Why haven't I kicked the bucket?
Well, I'll tell you why.

When mum was pregnant,
The doc said to my mum that
She'd got loads of time
Before the baby
(ME)
was ready.

The night I was born,
My parents were having a firework party
When the contractions started.
My dad's had a few beers,
But off we go to the maternity home.

When the old bill pulled Dad over
For going through a red light.
But when the copper found out
About my mummy and me
He took us to the maternity home
In the cop car.

When mummy and daddy got to the maternity home door
A nurse came out saying,

"Having babies is a b....y messy thing"

When the doc opened my mummy's tum
They found the umbilical
Wrapped round my neck.

So I wasn't breathing!

The doc did C.R.P. on me.
Finally, I started breathing again.
They put me in an incubator
For a week.
This was my lifeline,
One of lots.

My real lifeline is my parents
Who've got me where I am
Today.

Nikki had discovered Gymnastics and with two of her friends went to the local school for Gymnastics every Saturday. The PE teacher at Alresford school had told us she was also a very good sprinter. This came as something of a surprise as we had only ever seen her run in the "toddlers" races at Matt's sports days. She was selected to represent the school at the District Sports in the 100 metres. She made the final and ran very well obviously taking after her father!

Each year after that she represented her school at this event and she won by a large margin making quite a name for herself! Nikki was an all round athlete which meant she just cleaned up on every event on Sports Day. Some of the mums asked me to keep her at home on that day to give the other children a chance! How ironic was that!

Touch rugby was a new sport just coming into Primary schools. The PE teacher was a real exponent of the sport and his enthusiasm rubbed off on Nikki. She became captain of the school team, using her speed to great effect on the wing. The team won an Area schools cup competition with Nikki at the helm.

I am ashamed to say I found it very difficult to talk to Matt about Nikki's achievements fearful that it would be hard for him to take. But being Matt he was very proud of his little sister's success.

Nikki has since told me that Matt would encourage her all the way, telling her to do all these sports that he could never do, but he could take part by sharing in her success. Life was always about walking that narrow line. We could not allow Nikki to hide her light under a bushel just because her brother was disabled.

Socially Nikki was a very popular little girl always visiting friends after school or having them round to our house. I can honestly say all of her friends were totally accepting of Matt probably because they had known him all their lives. Not one of them was ever unkind or rude to him.

Barry:

ANOTHER ANECDOTAL EPISODE

At the grand old age of 44 I started playing football again, for Colchester United Veterans. Matt was highly amused by this as other than works five a side matches(in which I played out on the field) he had never actually seen me play in goal. So once again I was playing at Colchester United's Layer Road ground and Ipswich Town's Portman Road stadium against former football league stars.

One of the regular matches was Colchester United vets vs an Arsenal/Celebrity team in aid of charity. The last of these that I played in was in aid of the Colchester St Helena Hospice in front of a crowd of about 2000.

In amongst the ex Arsenal players, other sporting heroes of boxing cricket etc. was a sprinkling of pop stars and actors. One of the players was Ally Begg; singer with the boy band Bad Boys Inc, and now a Big Time TV Sports Host and presenter.

It was quite a wet night and the pitch was very slippy; anyway I had to go out to the edge of my penalty box to intercept a through ball. I dived on it and smothered it safely; the next thing I knew was a boot in the back from a very late challenge from an opponent. That day I had had a very very bad day at the office involving a massive row with my manager. I wasn't in a very forgiving mood. I got up and proceeded to kick the other player up in the air! It was Ally Begg(a hot headed Scotsman it turns out). An almighty scrap broke out between the two of us. Two of the Arsenal players including Gary Mason the former British Heavyweight Boxing Champion (sadly killed in a cycle accident) grabbed hold of me and restrained me. It took a bit longer before anyone grabbed Ally so he got a few more punches in at me!!

Once separated and some calm restored the referee sent us both off!! Then the Arsenal Manager (not Arsene Wenger!) marched onto the pitch saying this was the second successive match that Ally Begg had gotten into this sort of incident and that he would never play for Arsenal again. He then told the referee to rescind my sending off and allow me to carry on in the match! A very bemused ref grudgingly agreed and I continued and completed my final match, which we won.

Up in the stand watching all this happen were Matt and sister Nikki; apparently Matt was in hysterics laughing his head off whilst Nik was crying her eyes out at what was happening to her Dad!!

One of my team mates that night was Phil Coleman a former Colchester player and now head of PE at Matt's school!! Matt got a real hard time from him next day and for quite sometime after being teased about my antics. This also continued for Nikki once she started at the same school. Whenever Phil saw her coming towards him he would feign being hit and put his hands up in self defence whilst laughing his head off!

NIKKI'S MEMORIES OF THESE TIMES SHE DESCRIBES IN HER OWN WORDS:

As my mum has said throughout, my friends were, on the whole, accepting and kind to Matt. But I remember when inviting new friends round for the first time used to evoke some anxiety.

I felt obliged to warn them, "My brother is disabled so please don't be shocked."

I'm sure if any other siblings are reading this it will be a familiar memory.

During Matt's lonely teenage years my parents did everything they could to keep my life normal. It was normal, but I felt guilty a lot of the time, especially when my friends came to play or I was off out. In a way Matt's isolation made our relationship even stronger. I loved playing on his Nintendo even when winning meant a thump from Matt!

When he was lonely I never was; he'd play for hours in the garden with me, whether it was coaching my athletics, re-enacting "Due South", playing football or just pulling me along in a trailer behind his scooter.

Those are some of my happiest memories; I think it was probably here when I really became aware of Matt's handicap and loneliness.

Nikki talking about Matt pulling her behind his scooter reminds me of a trip to Clacton on one bright Boxing Day morning. Rollerblades were Nikki's main present that Christmas and to be honest she really was not that proficient on them, although it has taken me nearly twenty years to say it! Anyway the seafront in Clacton is nice and long and fairly smooth, just the place to practice your rollerblading!

Off we went, complete with Grandma. It was a lovely sunny morning after the previous very wet Christmas Day.

Matt was on his scooter, splashing through the puddles as he went. Before long he took pity on his little sister. She was putting an awful lot of effort into her skating but not really getting anywhere. Being the kind big brother that he is, Matt told Nikki to hold onto the back of his seat, pulling her along on her skates was clearly great fun and there were screams of delight from both kids.

All was going very well, until Matt went down a slope and, unfortunately and I hope accidently, took the bend at the bottom too sharply. Nikki let go and overtook Matt into a very large puddle!!

Her dignity was in tatters! Once we knew she was not hurt I'm afraid we were all, even Grandma, in stitches!

She was soaking wet and each time she tried to stand up the skates went in opposite directions and she ended up doing the splits!

Poor Nikki she still finds it hard to talk about it!

CHAPTER 41

GOOD AT GERMAN

I mentioned earlier Matthew's two best subjects at school were History and German.The First World War was the period of History they were studying for their O level exam. It was a period that Barry and I were also really interested in.

A school trip to the battlefields of Ypres was planned for the students and we were very keen for Matthew take part. The History teacher however had other ideas and told Matthew it would not be practical for him to go! She had of course reckoned without his mother. When I took her and her discrimination to task she made the very feeble excuse that such a long and gruelling day would be too much for him.

I contacted the company organising the tour and they told me that they were very experienced at accommodating people in wheelchairs. Furthermore with prior notice they would make sure Matt's going on the trip would not disadvantage the other students in any way. After my research Matthew was allowed to go. Barry went along as Matt's helper and there were several other dads accompanying the school party.

It was a long and demanding day but no one can fail to be moved by the Battlefields, cemeteries and memorials of the Great War and these youngsters were no exception. They all got so much out of it. It would have been unthinkable for Matt to have missed it.

German was another of Matt's best subjects which is quite amusing given his impaired speech, but despite this he got along with the language really well and still does to this day.

In August 1997, just before Matt started sixth Form College, we went to Majorca for our annual holiday, staying in the resort of Alcudia. It was a typical sun, sand sea and sangria family holiday. Matt wasn't keen; being a typical teenager he wanted to distance himself from his parents at every available opportunity. Yep you have all been there! It wasn't children being unkind that was the problem on this holiday, it was adults. Everywhere we went they tried to either push Matt out of the way or walk through him as if he wasn't there.

On one occasion, whilst visiting the caves of Drach and Ham, where it is quite dark and slippery, Matt was being pushed very hard in the back. Nikki was getting very angry about this and I'm not ashamed to say that two particular individuals returned to the Fatherland sporting very bruised shins!

One evening we walked into the neighbouring resort of C'an Pastilla and chose a restaurant, electing to dine alfresco. There were German couples either side of us carrying on a conversation together as if we didn't exist. We also became aware that we appeared to be invisible to the waiter. After a few minutes Matt insisted we leave. Despite our protests he was adamant so we got up and left. A safe distance away (bearing in mind we had rottweiller Nikki with us) Matt told us the two couples were saying that people like him should not be out in public. He had of course understood most of their conversation. How I wish he had had the confidence to speak to them, just imagine the look on their faces!

Now of course I must redress the balance and recount another incident on this holiday. We went to Palma for the day and it was extremely hot. Barry and I were finding it hard going getting Matt and his wheelchair up the many steps to the Cathedral. A young man approached and got hold of one end of the wheelchair and helped us carry it right to the top. We thanked him profusely and he told us it was no problem. As you have probably guessed the young man was German.

186

The inseparable pair: Bonnie and Freddie! 1993

Matt and helper at Schladming Austria in 1993

Gang of Six: from left to right; Jean and Barry, Wendy and Alan, Cheryl and Roger. 2007

From left to right: Matt Wendy Nikki and Barry 2006

A Magical and very special trio; Nikki, Grandma and Matt 2001

Alan and Ann's
Ruby Wedding
April 2006

CHAPTER 42

GCSE PASSES

As I explained earlier, before Matt could sit his GCSE's the Colne School contacted the Exam board to notify them they had a student with special requirements.

We had identified that Matt would need a scribe and also extra time for each exam and probably a separate location from the other students.

The Exam board agreed to all our requests but stipulated that if an exam spread over two days he would have to be kept apart from the other students. This did happen on one occasion and we had to have a teacher come and stay overnight to make sure Matt did not see or speak to another student. What irony!

The Headmaster very kindly gave up his office so that Matt could sit his exams without being disturbed. For his sacrifice he was richly rewarded with a giant Mars bar. Matt really wanted to go to the Sixth Form College in Colchester. He was confident he would be able to make friends and do well in a larger and less rural environment.

We had visited the College on their Open evening and, practically, it was possible. The Vice chancellor had been extremely helpful and told Matt that as long as he achieved at least 5   C grades or above in his exams, he saw no reason why he could not become a member of the college.

All Matt had to do now was make sure he got the grades. He did work very hard and my voice droned on and on throughout the house, one minute we were on the Western Front, the next I was narrating "An Inspector Calls". On results day accompanied by Carole and Gill he discovered his efforts had been rewarded with at least 5C's! Matt was thrilled and so were we.

The end of Matt's schooldays.

It meant saying goodbye to some marvellous people. Specifically Vic, his taxi driver who had been a diamond and had even on occasions taken Matt to Roots Hall in Southend in an effort to persuade him to support a "proper football team". Carole had been like a second mum and we will always feel grateful to her and her family.

The Colne School, although it hadn't all been plain sailing, had been mostly supportive.

But now a whole new chapter was beginning.

CHAPTER 43

SIXTH FORM COLLEGE

Gill was very keen to continue being Matt's helper as he started at the Sixth Form College. This was obviously a huge relief and gave Matt a more confident start. The Education Authority had agreed to finance his transport by taxi to and from college. Two major problems solved.

Matt met his new driver, a young man called Darren, a real "cheeky chappie", and they instantly hit it off. Darren teased Matt mercilessly about anything and everything but was always on his side; more about that later.

Gill planned to drive to our house and then go in the taxi with Matt to college. Darren's cab had ramps so it was easy for Matt's electric wheelchair to travel with him each day. Getting around the college was not a problem as there were plenty of lifts enabling Matt to access all parts of it. Everything was working out smoothly.

Before the term started Matt went to meet his Form Tutor, Liz Curry. At this point Matt didn't really know what he wanted to do other than maybe one day go to university and possibly do a journalistic degree.
Liz looked at Matt's O 'level results and saw the D for Maths. She gave him a hard stare and told him no university was going to accept him unless he had at least a C in this subject. Poor Matt, he loathed Maths but there was no way out of it and so Maths was included in his timetable. Little did he know then just how much that Maths class was going to change his life.

Liz has a terrific sense of humour and she and Matt were to become firm friends. Everything was in place for his start in September.

As Matt started college that September, Nikki was entering her last year of Primary school. Every year the Mercury theatre in Colchester puts on a pantomime. This particular year it was Dick Whittington and they were using local school children to be in the chorus. A team from the theatre came to Alresford School to conduct some auditions. Nikki was keen to try and was thrilled to be chosen along with two of her friends. Rehearsals began in September and so, together with Nikki's friend's parents, we worked out a rota to get the girls to every rehearsal and performance. The show started the week before Christmas and continued through January. It was quite a commitment but an unforgettable and enjoyable experience.

The practical arrangements we had put in place for Matt to start at sixth Form College were working well. He enjoyed his studies and college life. The only "downer" as far as Matt was concerned was his having to do the maths class. It wasn't long before he started talking about a young girl in his class called Shelley. She was very kind and friendly towards him and soon they were sharing lunches. Shelley introduced Matt to her boyfriend and their circle of friends.

I very clearly remember the first time I met Shelley.

Nikki and I had taken Matt into college to get the results of his maths exam. We waited in the car park as Matt had arranged to meet Shelley and get their results together. After about forty minutes I saw Matt coming round the corner about 100yards away accompanied by a young lady proclaiming in very loud Anglo Saxon that she had finally got her C in maths! Matt interrupted her flow and introduced us. I'm pleased to say we have been great pals ever since. One of Shelley's group that Matt got on particularly well with was a guy called Ben. Matt asked if he could invite Ben round for dinner one night; which he did. It was a Friday and after dinner Ben was

194

going to spend the evening with a group of friends at Shelley's house.

Ben phoned Shelley to find out what time and Shelley asked if Matt would like to come too. Barry took them the few miles to Shelley's house and then the plan was to put Matt in a taxi home. To most young folk this sounds so normal and unremarkable but for us it was "mega".

Barry and I waited up to help Matt and his wheelchair from the cab. Clearly he had had a great time. It was the start of Matt's social life, as from then on he was included in most of their activities. I don't think this group of Shelley, Steve, Helen, Nick, Ben, Dave, Tom and Amanda have any idea just how much they changed Matt's life.

Shelley's best friend was Helen and Matt first met her when she was a little tipsy and fell at his feet. Helen was of course the Helen I wrote about in chapter 5, Tony Windsor's daughter.

Matt had so many good times with them all. The general pattern was Barry or I would arrange where and when to meet them; they would collect Matt and wheelchair from us and then put him in a taxi at the end of the evening. One of us waited up to unload him and settle the fare. Most taxi drivers were very good and helpful but there are always exceptions. One driver refused to take him alone which put Matt and his friends to a lot of inconvenience.

At long last Matt had a circle of friends and a social life. It is probably fair comment that including Matt was not always easy and sometimes rather difficult but mostly he was just one of the gang. I remember Matt telling me about one particular night out.

The group had gone into town, Matt had his electric wheelchair. There is a very steep hill in Colchester called North hill and the story goes that, after a few drinks, the boys were pondering how fast Matt's chair would go down this hill. So propping Matt up outside the Estate Agents at the top they took it in turns to find out!

BARRY:

Sixth Form College introduced new more mature friends for Matt and some of the young men played football for various local teams. Matt started to go and watch them play on Saturdays and Sundays, thus keeping up the expansion of his social life. We had several gatherings at our house which ended up with them all playing football in the garden.

CHAPTER 44

MAKING CHANGES

In 1998 Barry and I decided to make a few changes to our lives.

For the previous two years I had been working as a dinner lady in Nikki's school and I was also doing voluntary work there, such as listening to the children read and taking groups of the older children to do some cooking.

Matt was settled at sixth form college and Nikki was in her last year at primary school so I decided the time was right for me to take on something more challenging. When I saw a vacancy advertised for a teaching assistant at a local special needs school, Market Fields, I applied. Luckily I got the job and my short term contract began in April 1998. 11 years later it is a job I still love and find very rewarding.

In August we went on a family holiday to Cyprus. Despite Barry's misgivings it was a great success. Matt and Nikki made lots of friends and had a wonderful time.

When we came back Barry had unfortunately contracted salmonella poisoning which meant he was off work for some time. Given this unexpected thinking time made him decide the time was right to leave the Prudential and strike out on his own as an Independent Financial Adviser.

Sadly for Matt his circle of friends, apart from Shelley, were all off to pastures new and the next exciting stage of their lives at University. They were scattered all over the country and although they met up during the holidays it was another chapter closed. It did however make Matt more determined than ever that he would get to University.

CHAPTER 45

THE GROIN STRAIN

Fantasy Football had become the latest craze and Matt was addicted. Retreating once more into his room he had also discovered the "web" and chat rooms.

In early 1999 he found out from someone at college and the internet that Chelsea FC had a thriving and very successful squad of disabled footballers who trained in Putney on Sunday afternoons. Matt persuaded Barry to take him along one Sunday to find out more about it. Once they arrived Matt was ribbed mercilessly for being a Manchester United supporter and a spastic. For some reason they felt that the second was a perfect qualification for the first! Despite all the ribbing the Chelsea boys made him very welcome. The players had wide ranging disabilities and before long Matt was wearing a Chelsea strip for their third team.
(A fact we were sworn to secrecy about.)

It was quite a commitment to make the long round trip to Putney every Sunday for training and matches but both Matt and Barry got a lot out of it. Unfortunately during one of the games Matt made a bad tackle and suffered what we thought was a groin strain. This put an end to his Chelsea days and began another long round of physiotherapy. Matt had a weekly session of physio for his "groin strain" at Colchester General hospital.

We were very regular visitors to this department, Nikki, whose athletics were going really well, had unfortunately picked up a hamstring injury, and so Barry's diary was once again full of physiotherapy appointments.

BARRY:

Whilst he was at sixth form college Matt spent the evening in the press box at Ipswich Town's Portman Road Stadium for their match against Stockport County. To get to the press box at Portman Road involved quite a trek and climb as it is at the very rear of the top of the then Pioneer stand! Matt's wheelchair was safely put away on the ground level. With help from me and the very friendly and obliging stewards he made the trip successfully. This was all covered in an article and picture in the Colchester Gazette the next evening. At this time journalism was Matt's main ambition.

Joining Chelsea FC Disabled football team through College and internet connections.

Matt was put in touch with Steve Keen who was running Chelsea FC. Disabled Team. He told Matt that he would be very welcome to join and come and train with them. Training was on Sundays early afternoon at Barn Elms Park, Putney, London --- a good 80 miles or so from our home! No satnav back in 2000 just a test for my navigational skills. The first session we attended was memorable for the very warm welcome Matt received; followed by merciless mickey taking from one of the players nicknamed "Squirrel". He took great pleasure in proudly announcing the arrival of Chelsea's first "MANCKY!" (Man United Fan) They were all great; very friendly and supportive and we made several trips to Putney prior to it all going wrong, as explained earlier by Wendy about Matt's "groin strain".

CHAPTER 46

LEGAL STUFF

In June 1999 our solicitors wrote and asked if they could come and visit us in our home. The purpose of the visit was for them to get to know Matt and establish a clear idea of Matt's life, his needs and level of care.

Barry and I were given the following tasks:

1) Identify all the areas of care we had given Matt because of his disability up to the present date and also details of the expenses we had incurred. Obviously this was specifically above and beyond what a non- disabled child would have required.

2) Forecast his future needs such as;

    a. Life expectancy
    b. Care
    c. Therapies
    d. Housing
    e. Aids and equipment

It was a mammoth and heart-rending task. Equipment and alterations to our home were relatively straightforward, but how do you quantify the all encompassing impact a disabled child has on family life? How do you separate the "normal" when you haven't known anything else? The answer is, of course, you can't.

All we could do was prepare a timetable of our daily lives past and present and separate the parts relevant to the disability. This we attempted to do over the following weeks. The meeting went very well and our solicitors were clearly impressed with Matt and all his achievements. After the meeting our solicitors wrote to say they were going to ask the defendant's solicitor for an interim payment. We could then immediately start making plans to enable Matt to have a better quality of life. The defendants had not admitted total liability but had agreed there was some fault on their part.

Unfortunately there is no "pause" button on life, and coping with the enormity of our situation and also everyday life was a physical and emotional juggling act. I apologise if I sound melodramatic but that is how it was.

Just like spinning plates.

CHAPTER 47

HUNG UP ON A NAIL

In August 1999 we were off to Florida again for another wonderful Disney holiday. The only downside was the pain Matt was experiencing with his groin. Walking and standing were very painful and increasingly difficult. Frequently his leg would give way and he would hit the deck. As he now weighed in the region of 10 stone it was physically tough especially for Barry. The following story I must include as it is one of Matt's favourites and a bête noire for Barry.

We were preparing to ride the Thunder Mountain Railroad in Disneyworld. Barry was helping Matt to get up from his wheelchair when Matt just collapsed taking Barry down with him. It was very hot and with energy levels low, Barry rounded on Matt in frustration, accusing him of not doing his exercises.

Matt's version is that Barry then hooked him up onto a nail by his shirt and walked away, leaving Matt dangling in abject agony from this nail! It sounds very funny now and has been embroidered greatly by our dangling son and heir.

I retrieved him from this "imaginary nail" (as if Disney would have such a thing!) and dusted him down. All Barry had actually done was prop Matt up against the wall! Nikki and I had to use our very best diplomatic skills to restore humour and harmony. Nikki recalls the incident very well.

Another holiday that springs to mind is the third Florida trip when Matt's hip troubles had surfaced. Matt enjoys exaggerating a story from this trip, so much so that I now remember it as he tells it, but I would just like to point out that the alleged pole and nail do not exist!

The episode did however provide the catalyst to exploring this groin strain further when we got back to England. The father of one of Matt's friends was a sports injury doctor so we made an appointment to see him. After an examination he sent Matt for an x-ray on his hip and pelvis. When we returned to his consulting room the previous jocular mood was replaced by one of shock and disbelief at what the x-ray had revealed.

In very basic layman terms Matt's right hip did not have a recognisable ball and socket joint. The socket looked more like a saucer, which meant each time Matt stood up his hip was dislocating. This was no football injury and was not going to be put right by any amount of exercise and physiotherapy. Matt was immediately referred to an Orthopaedic surgeon and at this point our two worlds collide.

Our negligence claim, up until now always in the background, exploded into overdrive.

Finding the right words to describe the ensuing months has seen me throw my pencil down in defeat so many times but, well, here goes.

To quantify the size of our claim, both sides instruct "expert witnesses". Their job is to provide a report for the Court, and if necessary give evidence in Court. Matt had to be examined, interviewed, assessed and judged both physically and mentally on every aspect of his life past, present and future. On occasions the same expert was instructed by both sides, as I have explained their duty was to the Court, it was down to the legal eagles to interpret the reports to whichever advantage.

Some of the experts came to our home but for others we had to travel long distances and all the time whilst these visits, reports and investigations were going on, Matt was studying for his A levels. Nikki's life also could not be put on hold.

Each report was like a building block that would eventually piece together and quantify our final claim. Forecasts required for his future included:

Care needs
Life expectancy
Earning potential
Health problems
Housing
Transport
Computer technology

Retrospective reports on the physical and very poignantly the emotional damage. Frustration was a hurdle Matt had had to overcome on a daily basis.

We were however shaken after reading one of the psychiatric reports and saw in black and white the levels of depression Matt had managed to hide from us, and I'm sure we will never know just how deep at times these feelings went. If ever we needed strength and fortitude as a family we were truly tested during this time. The final size of the claim is only numbers and time alone will tell if we got that remotely right. What cannot be included in those final numbers is the devastating impact one person's mistake or negligence can have on a life before it has begun.

As Matt's mum, I wish with all my heart I could turn back the clock and change that, and prevent it happening to somebody else. We all know that what happened to Matt can never be altered, but if writing this book and learning from our experiences helps in any way to influence or change existing practices in the future then job done!

CHAPTER 48

SURGERY

I need to backtrack here in order to move forward. As I said the x-ray of Matt's right hip revealed that his hip was dislocating when he tried to stand up. No amount of physiotherapy was going to put this problem right. Matt was referred to an Orthopaedic Surgeon and I took him along to his appointment on 11th November 1999. The Consultant Mr Shiv Shanker is a charming man, who was clearly horrified by Matt's x-rays. He told us the surgery Matt needed was beyond his capabilities, but he had done part of his training under the guidance of a man he thought could probably help.

The man in question was Mr Mark Paterson, a renowned Orthopaedic surgeon whose speciality was treating people with cerebal palsy. Mr Shiv Shanker said he would contact Mr Paterson on our behalf. Matt and I were deeply shocked and upset. We had hoped the solution was going to be a straightforward hip replacement but now it appeared to be far more serious.

Matt was still being seen by all manner of expert witnesses necessary to the ongoing progress of our compensation claim. Nikki's athletics and ensuing injuries also needed our attention and energy and of course everyday life goes on. It is extremely fortuitous that Barry had to keep a diary, not only for work commitments but all the other appointments going on in our life. His efficiency in keeping track of events has been invaluable to my writing this book and being able to relate the story as it unfolded. Never again will I complain about him being a hoarder!

Not only at this point was Matt in pain but his A levels were looming large on the horizon. The need for good results was essential to fulfill his dream of getting to university.

An Orthopaedic report by an expert witness was required for our claim. A stroke of luck came our way when the expert chosen by our solicitors was coincidentally Mr Paterson. An appointment was made for us to meet Mr Paterson at his consulting rooms in London on the 24th November 1999. Matt had compiled a list of questions and so, armed with this, we set off to London.

Mr Paterson was very charming and patient. He also recognized that on this visit he was wearing two hats as he called it. One hat as an orthopaedic surgeon to discuss Matt's hip problem and the other as an expert witness engaged for our compensation claim. He examined Matt very thoroughly and explained how his hip was dislocating. After this he took each of Matt's questions one by one.

I still have that sheet of paper with Matt's questions and my scribbled notes of Mr Paterson's replies, copied faithfully below.

QUESTIONS TO ASK

1. Will it hurt all the time after the op?

A> No! op will cure the pain.

2. How much movement will I have in the hip?

A> Turning round.

3. Will it be affected by the amount of sitting I do after the op?

A> No.

4. Will it deteriorate if I left it some years, say after University? If I wait does it corrode/ dissolve the hip?

A> Yes.

5. Anything that I can do to keep fit eg. swimming or will kicking make it worse?

A> Try and see.

6. Is my dislocating hip likely to cause any other complications eg. back, groin, hamstring?

A> Yes but they could be treated at a later date.

7. Anything I could take so my hip doesn't feel the cold so much?

A> No but try thermal underwear.
8. Is there a possibility that something could happen one day and I would be unable to move my leg, if so how quickly would I wait to have the op – an emergency?

A> Unlikely.

9. Is there a chance if I waited that people might find a better solution?

A> Not likely.

10. Is it possible to remove the hip and hip joint and replace with an artificial one?

A> High chance of dislocation. Too young and it would be short term success.

11. When I'm out of plaster what will I be like, will I need a lot of care, will I be able to use it straight away?

A> Hip cast, 10 days in hospital, splint for 6-8 weeks. 1st 3 weeks taking no weight, bed pans, 60% uncovered.

12. How tough will it be, if I fall over will it come apart?

A>20% chance

13. If I have the op and then later something better comes along could it be undone and then improved?

A>It can be repeated but if it's successful there would be no need.

14. Is the same thing likely to occur with my left hip?

A>Unlikely but not impossible. It has been compensating, so we'd screen both hips when under the anasthetic, possibly need minor soft tissue release.

15. Will I be able to stand up for long ?

A>Uncertain but op will cure pain.

As you can see Mr Paterson's answers were short but wholly honest!
In a nutshell Mr Paterson explained the awesome mechanics of the surgery:

1. Loosen off the muscles under the thigh.
2. Lengthen muscles from back, turn top of joint to remaining socket and screw in place.
3. Bring pelvic bone down to create a flap to prevent dislocation.

After the surgery.
Epidural painkiller, legs will be numb for 2-3 days, then reduce using other forms of pain relief as necessary. Preventing spasms will be a major concern. Length of op approx 3 hours.

It was a tremendous amount of information to take in. We received a copy of Mr Paterson's report a few weeks later. I include some extracts from it:

EXAMINATION
"Matthew Smith was alert and co-operative. He is clearly an intelligent young man." (Had to include that bit!)
"Clearly, Matthew is prevented from most of his weight-bearing activity by virtue of the pain in his right hip, and this in itself will reduce the risk of further subluxation. On the other hand, however, I believe that it is more likely than not that without treatment this hip will continue to be painful on a permanent basis."

"My recommendation would be for surgical intervention for this subluxing hip. This would be a major operation. It would involve extensive soft tissue releases, a varus femoral osteotomy, and some form of acetabular augmentation, effectively to deepen the socket. It would require a seven day stay in hospital, and a six week period in a hip spica. There is a peri-operative mortality from such procedures in cerebral palsy patients of up to as much as 1% and a 20% risk of repeat dislocation of the hip. In my opinion, there is no satisfactory alternative to surgery."

As you can see it was a major operation and a huge decision for Matt to make, but there really was no alternative.

Matt agreed to have the surgery immediately after his A- levels the following July. His recovery he was confident would be complete before the start of the semester and more importantly "Freshers"!!!

Meanwhile life goes on and we all had a lot of living to do.

CHAPTER 49

WHICH UNIVERSITY?

The first item on our agenda came a few days after our trip to London. It was an open day at Lincoln University. Lincoln was the first prospective university that Matt visited. I have to say we were very impressed. The specially adapted accommodation really was all it claimed to be! The campus and facilities were brilliant.

Lincoln is a beautiful city and purely from a "mum" point of view not a million miles from home. I could really envisage Matt going there.

So all Matt had to do was get the right grades in his A-levels, sail through major surgery and complete his recovery by mid September. Piece of cake!! Matt was also keen to check out Preston University and Stafford University in Stoke on Trent. In February he and Barry took a trip up north to have a look. Matt was very impressed, but from a purely practical point they were both non starters.

Stafford was the same distance from home as Lincoln, but the cobbled streets meant a very bumpy ride for Matt especially after major surgery. Preston was great but pure distance alone, a round trip of 600 miles, meant we would struggle to get there and back in a day should an emergency arise. Lincoln was therefore the number one choice.

CHAPTER 50

BATTLE TOUR

In the February half term we had booked an "In Flander's Fields" battlefields tour. As I have already said The Great War is an interest we all share as a family. It was my first time to visit the battlefields of the Western Front. The trip was great and so moving but the pain and lack of mobility Matt was experiencing meant he missed out on the complete tour. It was added to his list of "to do's" post operation.

The trip however still made a huge impact on him and Matt will tell you that everyone should experience a trip to Delville Wood.

I asked Matt to explain in his own words why he feels this way;

Matt:

DELVILLE WOOD:

I've experienced many weird things (probably not all paranormal!)

But when I went on a World War One battlefield tour to the Somme with my parents and Nikki in February 2000 I had one of the most profound experiences of my life to date.

A part of the tour took us to Delville Wood, known as "Devil's Wood", which is situated near to the village of Longueval. The site is now owned by South Africa as they purchased it from the original owner following the end of the Great War. It was the site of a ferocious battle which commenced in 1916, involving nearly 4,000 South African troops. The wood is now a permanent memorial to commemorate the brave men who fought there. In Delville

Wood today there still remain the bodies of many of the fallen that were never recovered and buried in a proper cemetery.

The wood itself was completely flattened during the war, apart from one Hornbeam tree which still remains, albeit bullet ridden. Anyway the wood has recovered and it is peaceful and tranquil.

At the time of our trip, I suffered with a dislocated hip so I was wheelchair bound, the trench systems still remain which you can walk through but unfortunately I could not. My parents and sister wanted to do this walk so they left me sitting by the bullet ridden Hornbeam tree which is situated at a trench entrance. I am no hippy but the feeling I had sitting by the tree, I cannot explain, apart from the feeling of being euphoric and at one with everything, a true sense of belonging. I sat there for a good fifteen minutes before my parents and sister came back to collect me.

When we got back on the coach this elderly man with his wife and son said to me, "I have never seen a wild deer come up and stand by a person before, that must have made your day".

To which I responded, "What deer?"

The man said, "The one standing next to you for at least two minutes; you could not have missed it, it was about a foot away!"

I was bemused and thought him a bit of a fruitcake, until another man who had been listening said; " Excuse me, but it was a Springbok Gazelle!"

By now I thought we were sitting on the wrong bus! I was expecting men in white coats coming to take them away he! he! Springbok gazelles in France! Or a deer stood by me! What drugs were in those woods? As the coach left our tour guide told us a bit more about the battle and that to boost the morale of the South African troops a springbok gazelle named Daisy had been sent over as a mascot. The tour guide was always the last one to get on the bus so would not have heard the earlier accounts. I think at least six people, myself included were in a state of shock and disbelief. If the man who had said it was a springbok gazelle knew the story then that may dull the experience, I am physically disabled but there is nothing wrong with my eyesight, so even if it was not a springbok, don't you reckon I would still have noticed a deer standing a foot away from me! I would like to remember those who fought and died in the "Great War", we will never forget them.

Just as a postscript to Matt's story, there is a little museum beside Delville Wood and "Daisy's" arrival is well documented.

On this trip Matt also had the experience of "Going over the top!"

We visited Beaumont Havel and Newfoundland Park, where you can walk through a lot of the frontline trenches. The original "duckboards" have been replaced and so we thought it would be accessible for Matt in his wheelchair. Unfortunately the trench narrows and we could get no further forward, as there were many people behind us we couldn't go backwards either so we had no choice but to go "over the top!"

I don't intend this remark to appear flippant but the experience was not wasted on us.

CHAPTER 51

MORE SKIING

"A" levels were racing towards Matt and to ensure that he had the time he needed to complete each exam the Exam Board required a letter from our GP confirming his needs to be genuine to qualify for extra time and, if necessary, a scribe. Dr Snell had retired and so Matt was seen by another partner. This doctor became very interested in Matt. His own son was a doctor practising in London and living a stone's throw from the hospital where Matt was going to have his hip surgery.

When this young man was told about Matt he very kindly offered Barry and me accommodation during Matt's stay in hospital.

Back to the exams, and so with the letter from our GP and the whole-hearted support from the sixth Form College everything was in place for Matt to sit his "A" level exams.

An "interim" payment from the Defendants had been forthcoming which enabled Matt to make some changes to his life. He had been assessed by various IT experts and was now able to buy some equipment. He could now advertise for and pay a carer to take him out socially. Although actually recruiting someone suitable was not easy as Essex seemed to be a "blackhole" for recruiting carers.

The Uphill Ski Club was going to the USA in March that year and so Matt booked himself on the trip, Alan again going as his "buddy". In fact Alan was now such an old hand at these trips he was made Group leader. Unlike previous times with the USC Matt was now confined to a wheelchair which meant he had to use a "bi ski". No charging down a mountain with his hands between his knees this time. The trip was a great experience but it again poignantly underlined how much Matt's life was being restricted by his hip problem.

CHAPTER 52

SWEDEN

Youthful curiosity and, I feel sure, an element of fear that he would not survive the surgery, or that its level of success would be below his expectations, Matt wanted to experience Sweden.

The country's reputation for being very accessible and benevolent towards disabled folk was something he was keen to discover for himself. In the Easter holidays he employed a friend to accompany him as a carer. The trip was an experiment to see how Matt was going to manage life with paid carers. Barry and I were going too but purely as a "back up". We had to agree to interfere only when invited to!

Nikki was off Skiing in France with her school at the same time. We set off for Stockholm via Stansted Airport. Matt's first obstacle came in the Ryanair departure lounge. He had sailed through check in. No comment had been made about his wheelchair. The lounge was full of Swedish folk, who took no notice of Matt at all. But when it came to boarding the clerk on the desk asked in a very derisive voice exactly how Matt was planning to get on the plane. Apparently he should have accessed the plane from the ground floor of the airport. There was no time for this now and so he would not be able to fly!

Having requested airport assistance when the trip was booked we were understandably very upset. There was a lot riding on this holiday and the prospect of falling at the first fence was just too much. The official's total lack of helpfulness and the manner in which she was speaking to Matt attracted the attention of the erstwhile dis-interested Swedes. They approached the desk as a group and asked what the problem was. After being

217

almost gleefully told by the official that Matt could not board the plane as he couldn't get up the aircraft steps, and the specially adapted ramp was in another part of the airport. They replied "No problem" they would help carry Matt and chair up the aircraft steps. Her face was a picture! And that is exactly what they did! They disappeared into the aircraft afterwards as if it was an everyday occurrence.

Sweden was lovely. We all had a great time. We didn't see much of the boys except at meal times. After they discovered the local night clubs, breakfast wasn't a meal we shared. One evening Barry and I walked into Gamla Stan, the old part of Stockholm. It's very pretty, very old with lots of brightly painted buildings and an abundance of good restaurants. We chose one in which the main dining area was way down in the cellars. During our meal Barry told me that behind my right shoulder there were four men eating, one of whom was very familiar. I tuned in and the voice was unmistakable. It was Arsene Wenger (Arsenal F.C Manager). There's just no getting away from football!

The trip proved that with Matt's current level of disability one carer was not enough, especially when it came to getting him in and out of vehicles. It gave us food for thought and highlighted several areas that would need serious attention for Matt to become independent of us.

We returned home from Sweden the night before Nikki was due back from her skiing trip. I got a phone call from her early the next morning. She didn't sound quite her usual bubbly self and I put this initially down to tiredness. Our conversation went along the lines that although she had a brilliant time I wasn't to panic when we met her! (Don't you just love that!)

It transpired she had taken a tumble and hurt her elbow but, Nikki being Nikki, had picked herself up and carried on skiing. When the pain had got too much she was taken to hospital, where an x-ray showed her elbow was broken.

The French hospital staff put a very sophisticated brace on it. It would however mean months of physiotherapy once the brace was removed. We were certainly doing our best to keep the National Health physiotherapists busy. C'est la vie!

In May Barry, Nikki and I went up to Hull to visit Jean and Peter. Matt was staying at home and employing a friend to be his carer, gaining more practical experience for the future. We had a lovely weekend in Hull and before we left we had planned to have Sunday lunch in Jean and Pete's local.

I had a walk down their garden to make a fuss of the labrador next door. Unfortunately, I tripped, (this was before the pub!) My foot swelled up, it was so painful that I knew I had done a number on it.

During the drive home I was able to keep ice packs on my foot but my trip to casualty the next day revealed it was broken in two places. Plastered and on crutches I was at the mercy of Matt and his generosity in sharing his toilet and shower facilities with me. Payback time!

All the previous years of (mostly imagined I'm sure) nagging and whip cracking was remembered and used at every available opportunity.

I was constantly told "Of course you can manage, just put a bit more effort into it!" His poking fun at my disability was equalled only by my own frustration. What a team we were, Nikki's arm in a brace, Matt in a wheelchair and me on crutches. It took forever to load us all into a car.

CHAPTER 53

A LEVELS

To help with quantifying Matt's compensation claim we thought a visit to a Naidex exhibition would be useful. It was a "look see" at what was on the market for people with disabilities. There was an exhibition being held at the NEC in Birmingham and so Barry, Matt and I went along. There were stands galore; every conceivable aid was exhibited, but the prices!

Adaptive equipment for disabled folk really is a license to print money. It made us feel very angry to see that there is an aid to overcoming most practical problems, but at tremendous financial cost.

Matt was particularly interested in mechanised wheelchairs, and so we arrived at a stand exhibiting the "Trax". This machine looked truly remarkable. A luxury armchair on wheels! The expandable wheel base meant it could cope with all manner of obstacles and terrain.

An arena had been set up with kerbs, bridges, slopes and rough ground. Matt was very keen to have a test drive and before long he attracted quite an audience as he put the machine through its paces, he earned a round of applause at the end of his final circuit. The Trax was the same price as a Ford Escort, but as he would never be able to drive one of those, this machine represented quite a chunk of independence.

We booked a demonstration and test drive at our home. Matt loved it and ordered one without delay! He really put the machine through its paces, especially when out with us and the dogs, Nikki had to jog to keep beside him, it was beneficial training for her too! To this day he still drives it around the countryside of his Lincolnshire home. The exhibition gave us some good ideas and areas to explore to maximize Matt's quality of life and independence.

It was now June 2000 and as I see by Barry's efficient diary keeping ,there was no slowing down our pace of life. Appointments and meetings surrounding Matt's future were still coming thick and fast. Another visit was paid to Lincoln University and happily Matt's application was accepted with conditions.

The nuts and bolts of the claim were now in place. We went to London and the Inns of Court to meet the QC and his team who would represent us in resolving Matt's case. What an impressive experience! Parts of the Inns are so old and steeped in tradition it is like stepping back in time. Our QC and barrister had minds so razor sharp they cut through pages of reports like a knife through butter. They asked questions, picking up on some of the most minute detail. We could only marvel at the computer like brains these men had. I was very concerned we would feel intimidated by such expertise, but my fears were groundless as they were also very charming and clearly impressed with Matt. So glad they were on our side!!

In the meantime A-levels! Gill became an almost permanent fixture in our home as Matt prepared for these all important exams.

The Sixth Form College had finalised the arrangements and conditions set by the exam board. It was a stressful time as it is for anyone but of course Matt was also in pain and had major surgery to look forward to. After each exam Matt was unhappy and felt he hadn't done very well, but that's pretty normal too. It was all in the lap of the gods and all we could do now was wait.

CHAPTER 54

THE OPERATION

The days were rapidly counting down to his surgery, which was scheduled for Monday 10th July. His last exam took place on Friday the 7th July, so he had a whole weekend in which to let his hair down.

We had several things to sort out first. Primarily after his surgery and post op care in London he had to be admitted into a hospital in Colchester. The nature of the plaster cast which would encase him from waist to toe and with his legs kept wide apart meant we couldn't get him into our house! So in hospital he would have to stay until the cast came off. We arranged for him to go into the Oaks, a private hospital in Colchester for about 6 weeks; it actually turned out to be eleven weeks.

Nikki was also going through a hard time; a boy at her school had been bullying her and making comments about her "spastic" brother.

Barry and I met with her form tutor and year manager who promised to deal with the bully. We also made them aware of the worrying time she was having with her brother. So with all this in mind we planned that, after the first couple of days in London, one of us would be back in Alresford each night to keep life as normal as possible. Enter again our ever supportive family and friends, Alan, Ann, Philip, Pauline, Colin, Lynne and Tony were all willing to drive back and forth to London to visit Matt and to ferry me back and forth. We can never thank them enough for their unstinting love and support.

Barry was trying to continue working as much as possible for we still had bills to pay. Fortunately I was given compassionate leave from school.

On 10th July, the ever stoical and loving Grandma was in place to look after Nikki, and the dogs were in kennels for ten days. As Barry, Matt and I headed off to the London Independent Hospital in Stepney. Matt was in very good spirits and bravely hid his fear.

We arrived at the hospital and were met by Mr Paterson and the nursing team who would be looking after Matt. Mr P went through the surgery plan again. The mechanics of it all made me shudder, but Matt was in jocular mood, wisecracking with Mr P and the nurses.

First he was going to have a chest x-ray and then blood tests. As soon as the words blood tests were spoken Matt said "Right; that's it I'm off, nobody said anything about blood tests before!" Never had I felt so proud of this brave young man. Again that wicked sense of humour appeared.

Matt was prepped for theatre and after we had said the usual goodbyes and good lucks Barry and I were shown to a room where we were to sit and wait for the next five hours.

I remember trying to watch a film about the turbulent life of Tina Turner, but concentration was not at its sharpest, my thoughts were more "river deep" and my prayers that Mr P was "simply the best." Some hours later we were told Matt's operation was over and he was back in his room.

Mr P came to see us with the good news that the surgery had gone well and there had been no horrible surprises. The biggest problem was going to be keeping Matt still. He was sedated to help prevent any involuntary movements and muscle spasms.

Barry and I went into Matt's room. He was lying completely flat, and surrounded with drips and machinery. The background music I thought was playing was the "beeps" from all the machinery.

Both his legs were plastered from hip to ankle with a "broom handle" inserted into the plaster between his knees to keep the hips at the right angle. He was obviously heavily sedated and on morphine but he knew we were there and he was able to speak a little.

Mr P said he would come back in the morning. Barry and I were given a room along the corridor so that we could sleep if we wanted to.

We phoned a very anxious Nikki with the good news and spent the night in Matt's room. Mr P came back the next morning and showed us the x-rays. He was very pleased with what he referred to as his "carpentry" The most important thing now was to try and raise Matt's head and shoulders little by little so the anaesthetic would not settle on his chest, and more importantly, as far as Matt was concerned, so that he could watch the cricket on TV.

As everything appeared to be going well Barry went home and I planned to stay for the next two nights.

Matt was "twitching" a lot with the inevitable spasms. The harder he tried to stop the worse the spasms became, he needed a diversion.

I had discovered that reading aloud to him helped. He was so used to hearing my voice drone on that invariably he fell asleep and his twitching stopped.

All was going well until I noticed Matt's morphine was getting low. The nursing shift had changed so I mentioned the low morphine to the oncoming nurse, but she said it was fine. Shortly after this Matt became agitated and said he was in a lot of pain, he pleaded with me to get help and I hit the panic button. The morphine had run out!

A nurse from the intensive care unit was sent for and she immediately replaced the morphine but until it kicked in Matt was in agony. He was in so much pain they were unable to raise his shoulders. Mr P was summoned and when he arrived he was most unhappy. Matt had had muscles cut and bones sawn through and was now able to feel every bit!

It was very harrowing but by the time Barry came back that evening with Nikki and Grandma Matt was stable and calm restored. Apart from that one hiccup the nursing staff were marvellous and had obviously taken a real shine to Matt, some of them even popped in to visit him on their day off. I spent one more night in Matt's room and then was happy to relinquish my vigil to Barry. The prospect of going home to Nikki and sleeping in my own bed was very appealing.

Once home I spent the evening with Nikki and Grandma. I had lots of phone calls to make to family and friends all anxious for news of Matt's progress. Very late that night I had a phone call from Barry. It began with those immortal words, "Please don't panic".

Matt was now stable, but earlier he had developed a severe reaction to the morphine and we had almost lost him. Barry had noticed things were not right, Matt's temperature had been rapidly rising, which was treated with paracetamol and then Matt's breathing became erratic at which point Barry hit the panic button. Matt's room was invaded by doctors and nurses as Matt slipped into unconsciousness. Barry remembers the nurses saying "Come on Matthew" and himself pleading with Matt to come back.

Barry was told to hold Matt's hand and keep talking to him. He told Matt, "Please mate, mum has left me in charge and she'll kill me if anything happens!" Medical skill saved the day and Matt opened his eyes. Barry looked up and through his tears saw the whole team crying tears of relief. That boy certainly knows how to keep us on our toes!

BARRY:

As I recall it: the "relaxed and peaceful" build up to Matt starting at Lincoln University.

Following on from Matt's "groin strain" and the subsequent trips to see Mark Paterson, have X-rays, MRI scans etc, the time came for Matt's admission to the London Independent Hospital in Stepney. The operation was a success and initially all was well with Matt's post op recovery. After a couple of days we decided that Wendy should return home and for me to stay with Matt.

Because of Matt's C.P. he was unable to operate the pain relief clicker for the morphine so dad was the one to press the button. We had been told that you couldn't overdose using this medication dispenser!

Although in some discomfort Matt was doing okay until about 9pm on the first night when I was on sole parental duty! About this time I noticed that his breathing was becoming laboured and that he was quite unresponsive, almost unconscious. I pushed the panic button and within minutes the room was full of doctors and nursing staff. They were pleading with Matt to respond and asked me to keep talking to him. His temperature was soaring and Nurse Hyacinth administered a paracetamol suppository. All this time I was pleading with Matt to wake up and talk to me, cos if he didn't his Mum would kill me!

Eventually (it seemed like a lifetime) Matt's breathing became less laboured and his temperature lowered considerably. His return to consciousness was greeted with huge relief by all the medical staff in attendance but nowhere near the level of relief his dad felt.

It transpired that Matt had got pneumonia and although he had not overdosed on morphine it had affected his breathing levels and that was what caused the really scary crisis that night.

Of course all of this treatment was private medicine at work, as was Matt's twelve weeks' convalescence at the Oaks Private Hospital in Colchester. By the time the surgery and post op care had happened Matt had been awarded an interim payment following Essex Rivers Health Authority's admission of Liability. What would have happened without any private funding Heaven only knows. I was so grateful for the fact that seven years earlier, when my Prudential career was in danger of going belly-up, that a visiting branch manager had given me Robert Longhurst's number and that I had kept it. The Prudential manager in question had used Lorimer Longhurst and Lees in connection with a medical negligence case on his disabled daughter's behalf. That number and our subsequent contact with Robert Longhurst was absolutely pivotal in us proceeding with Matt's claim.

Nikki:

I have included a piece of English coursework Nikki wrote at this time.

My stomach's churning. People all around me are standing staring at me. My hand is shaking but it's not because I'm cold. I turn to run away but my exhausted parents grab me by my arm to stop me from running. They edge me forwards. I look at the tired expressions on their faces. It's like one of those dreams where the walls are closing in on you and you are trying to wake up but it seems to take forever.

All around me phones are ringing. People are sitting on chairs all with the same worried expression on their faces. The air is warm. I reached forwards to twist the cold steel handle.

227

As I open the door, my aunt and uncle arriving interrupt me. I close the door and go to see them. They are both wet to the bone and look as if they have been stranded at sea for a week. It's like the monsoon out there my uncle Mick mumbled. "You alright kid? Have you been in yet?"

"No." I replied. "I've spent the past twenty minutes trying to pluck up the courage when you arrived," I snarled coldly.

"Would you like us to come in with you?"

I told them how I would go in my own time but I was not to prevent them from going in. They were gone for forty minutes. My bottom had gone numb from sitting on the uncomfortable plastic chairs. I read the same smoking poster over and over again. I thought if I read it one more time I would go mad. I even stared at the clock no end of times! The forty minutes they were gone seemed like forever. When my aunty and uncle finally came out the room they looked sad and worried. My throat tightened as I asked what was wrong. They ignored my question and said your mum and dad asked if you are ready yet? I said firmly, "No!"

My uncle Mick is a laid back easygoing man. Nothing bothers or gets him down, but this obviously did. Things must look bad. They went off to the cafeteria. They were gone a long time. I thought to myself, it's not that I do not want to go in it's just that I need to prepare myself first. I tried to picture the tubes and machines so that when I saw them I wouldn't freak out. My aunty and uncle came back carrying three teas and two coffees. They handed me a coffee with milk and two sugars and asked if I was ok. They opened the plastic door that was made out to be wooden but definitely wasn't! They came out looking distressed, they looked like they had just seen a ghost. My aunty's lip was quivering, my uncle stared longingly into his tea. It was obvious they were trying to hold themselves together for my sake. Where my uncle had been breathing deeply his glasses had steamed up, he pushed them off the end of his nose and gave them a quick clean and returned them to his face. Aunty Joyce went to lift her tea to her mouth when her hand started to shake and the tea fell through her fingers. Frantically she dropped to the ground mopping the teas from the uncarpeted floor with her cotton handkerchief.

There was a long silence. I asked what was wrong. They both spoke at once. I asked again. My aunty stared down at the floor and mumbled nothing is wrong.

"That's it", I said, "if you won't tell me what's going on I'll go in and see for myself". As I slowly silently walked down the long dark virtually silent corridor my heart was pounding. I was freezing cold but covered in sweat. My stomach was fluttering like a thousand butterflies. I turned a corner in the smelly dingy corridor. I walked in time with my heart. I finally reached room one o nine.

I took a deep breath and opened the door. I peered round slowly, I walked over to the bed where my brother was laid. My mum and dad were sat beside him clenching his right hand. Their faces lit up when they saw me. They coaxed me closer as I was about two or three metres away from the bed. They told me that he couldn't speak but he could hear me, why don't you tell him about your day? I nervously cleared my throat. At the time I didn't know why I was nervous though in hindsight I know now. The walls were very high and white and plastered with various get well soon cards, though he had only been in hospital one day as he had his operation yesterday July the tenth. I will remember that day forever. I had been dreading this day for months ever since he had been having physio for a suspected hip strain from playing football for Chelsea disabled club. Later found to be a disaster waiting to happen from birth.

I began to tell him about my day. I began by telling him all my friends had made a get well soon card for him. I told him how I got into my first ever fight because a boy I knew stood up in front of my whole maths class and announced to them you were going to die on the operating table. He wasn't even supposed to know you were even in hospital. I told Matt how I had this boy pinned to a wall as I thought that that was the sort of thing that he would find funny. I found it very difficult to have a one-way conversation but soon became accomplished at it.

Every five minutes his face would wince so mum or dad would push a button that would pump morphine into his body. There was a knock at the door and in came the consultant with my aunty and uncle who came to say they were going to go home. The consultant Mark Patterson came to tell us the operation had been successful "my best work this year" he smiled. "We built a whole new hip socket we took bone from his pelvis so now his hip won't dislocate. He should even be able to walk a few steps. The one thing I can guarantee is he will be pain free". That was music to our ears!

Mum and I made our way home and my dad stayed at the hospital with Matt. Later that evening mum and I received a phone call, it was dad ringing from the hospital, I have some bad news. My heart sunk to my shoes. Mum's face dropped. "We nearly lost Matt tonight, the valium and morphine had settled on his chest and given him pneumonia. He fitted and stopped breathing. It was pretty hairy. He was out for a long time. I was demanding him to speak to me when he squeezed my hand and started breathing again. He's stable now but still has a very high temperature.

Mum and I left early the next morning and arrived at the London Independent a little after eleven o'clock. Dad was smiling which was a good sign. He woke up this morning and said, "I'm hungry!" He ate two slices of toast. He's a bit more with it today! I was expecting to have a normal conversation with him but every five minutes he'd drift off to sleep. He only had sixteen weeks until he had to go to Lincoln University. That was if he passed his A-levels. We were still anxiously waiting for the results. Every now and then he would squeeze my hand as if to say "I'm listening!" At about one o'clock his best mate Shelley arrived. As soon as she saw Matt and all of the machines she burst into tears. I was really surprised. I had never seen an adult cry other than on the television before. I couldn't believe it; I didn't understand.

Looking at my second year brother who is studying at Lincoln University it's hard to believe his operation was only a year ago. He can even walk a few paces. Mind you the only thing he can actually remember about being in hospital is going into hospital. He came out of hospital with only five weeks to spare. He is going to turn twenty-one in three weeks time. He can't even remember Rose the nurse he really fancied!

So with a pinch of exaggeration and a spoonful of licence Nikki managed to get a good mark for her English coursework, it wasn't all bad!

BACK TO THE REAL LIFE DRAMA.

Matt's recovery had taken a slight backward step. Raising his head and shoulders was still essential to clear the anaesthetic from his chest, but despite our best efforts and a hydraulic bed unfortunately he developed pleurisy. Strong antibiotics were prescribed and the doctor also recommended we get Matt out into the fresh air.

There is a little square of gardens just opposite the hospital and so, with the help of a nurse and a porter we managed to manoeuvre Matt, complete with bed and drips out into the car park for a few minutes. The gardens, although just across the road, were going to be much more of a challenge! After a couple more days

Matt was almost sitting upright, well upright enough for us to consider getting him into a wheelchair.

The hospital had a chair we could borrow and it had extendable legs to accommodate heavily plastered limbs. Matt's cast was so large that even this chair was going to require some DIY. Fortunately there was a hardware shop just along the main road and so Barry, armed with some of Matt's vital statistics, paid them a visit. He managed to get a piece of wood cut to the right size and shape to fit under the heavy plaster.

That was the easy bit, the next job of getting Matt off his bed and onto the wheel chair was going to be much more difficult. It took the help of several strategically placed nurses, plus Barry and me to lift him from the bed and onto the chair without disturbing all his drips and tubes! Each attempt became a little easier and soon we had it down to a fine art. We made it into the gardens every day.

London was very hot that July but it was going to take a lot more than sunshine to put some colour back into those cheeks. Shelley, Helen and Ben came to visit. The girls walked into Matt's room and then both ran out crying because he looked so ill. After taking a couple of minutes to compose themselves they went back in and did a great job lifting his spirits. After 10 days Mr P was satisfied Matt could be transferred back to the Oaks hospital in Colchester and into Dr Shiv Shanker's care. The nursing staff in London gave Matt a tremendous send off and with me travelling back in the ambulance with him we headed back to Colchester and the next stage of his recovery.

CHAPTER 55

THE OAKS

When we had all arrived at the Oaks and Matt was safely installed in his room, the sister arranged a little meeting between us and the nursing staff. It was a kind of "get to know you" exercise. It gave us a chance to tell them a bit about Matt and the sort of help he was going to need. We didn't give them too much information; after all we wanted them on side!

Barry planned to stay with Matt that first night, and then we would take each day in shifts between us. This was until Matt and the staff had got to know each other. Matt's speech had deteriorated whilst he had been so poorly and so we couldn't expect total strangers to understand him immediately. He was going to be a guest of the hospital for several weeks so it was important to make his stay a pleasant one for everyone.

Barry and I took it in turns to be there at meal times to feed him, which obviously was a big help to the staff. It wasn't long before all the staff had warmed to Matt. As usual his wicked sense of humour had won through. During their breaks they would pop in and have a little chat or share a joke. The doctors were regular visitors knowing full well Matt would be watching the cricket and they could catch the latest score! The night staff always included him when ordering their late night snacks from the nearby McDonalds.

One nurse remembers the first time she was looking after Matt; she gave him a wash and was then going to clean his teeth. Not being familiar with his electric toothbrush she asked him what to do (big mistake!) Matt told her to hold the brush head facing towards her, put the toothpaste on and switch on. She did exactly as she was told and was plastered in toothpaste! A huge giggle rose from the prone young man and battle lines were drawn!

Matt had complained that he wasn't allowed to use the inner courtyard garden to sit in when the weather was so hot. The nurses explained that there was a family of ducks in residence, and they didn't want to disturb this family and their young brood. Matt still protested that this wasn't fair as he was paying far more than the ducks for his accommodation! Each time the dinner menu came round Matt requested roast duck. His request was granted one night when the staff substituted his meal with a rubber duck! The nurses took their revenge whenever possible, Water was their main weapon and Matt took a soaking "accidently" on several occasions. His reply was a "super soaker" which he hid under the covers, but of course with his poor aim he inevitably came off worse.

Being back in Colchester meant Matt had a lot more visitors. Because he could now sit up, under garments were required. Being completely unreasonable Matt refused to wear a skirt!
The nature of his plaster meant we couldn't slide anything up his legs, so a little fashion designing was needed. I bought several pairs of cotton boxer shorts, unpicked the side seams and sewed several lengths of tape to each side.

The back of these shorts went under his butt, the front was up between his legs and laced at the sides. They were stunning! But I don't think he has ever worn boxers since.

A steady supply of family and friends helped to relieve the boredom and keep Matt in good spirit. Cheryl lived very close to the Oaks so she often popped in on her way to Asda. Tim came every Friday and played monopoly. Bonnie and Freddie were also regular visitors when we could get Matt outside in the evenings. It was mostly the afternoons Matt found long and tedious. The nurses always knew when he hadn't any visitors because he pressed his bell more often. Now that he was feeling better it was basically a waiting game until the plaster came off. The physiotherapists visited him regularly rubbing their hands in anticipation at the torture they promised to unleash once the plaster was off.

Another visitor was Christopher Purchase, the QC representing us in our compensation claim. Accompanied by our solicitor we spent an entire morning discussing details and fine-tuning some of the financial aspects. It was a very productive and worthwhile meeting and Matt's fan club had increased again.

The next big entry in the diary was Thursday 17th August and the A level results. It's a nail-biting time for anyone but Matt had built his whole recovery around these results. Bob Eden, the vice principal of the Sixth Form College, came to the hospital with the all important document, Matt was devastated, 2D's.

Bob had however already been in touch with Lincoln University. In consideration of the circumstances which surrounded Matt taking his A levels, along with his good O level results, they were still keen to offer him a place. All Matt had to do now was get out of plaster, work like mad at his physiotherapy and be fit in time for the start of the term. No problem!

On Wednesday 23rd August I stayed with Matt all day waiting for his plaster to be removed. Finally, after what seemed an eternity the technician arrived and after much sawing and cutting the plaster was off.

What did I do as we looked down at Matt's legs? Did I offer words of positive encouragement? No, I cried. As I have said Matt's legs were thin but the two little white sticks revealed to us now were so pathetic I could not believe they would ever look like real legs

236

again! Matt said it felt really strange without the plaster and he did laugh when he saw his "new" legs.

There was one silver lining; no more designer boxers! The next morning the physiotherapists were unleashed and in Matt's words the torture began. From memory their first objective was to get some movement in the knees and build up the wasted muscles. They visited Matt every morning, working on him and then showing him exercises he could do as he was lying in bed. He worked really hard, if the physiotherapists asked him to repeat an exercise say 15 times, Matt would push himself to do 30.

Now that he was out of plaster the medical staff thought it would be beneficial for us all if Matt came home for weekends. We were over the moon, but apprehensive about how we would cope, anxious not to make a mistake in case we caused him damage or pain. With my track record it was a real worry. Matt had been in hospital now for eight weeks and had undoubtedly become a bit "institutionalized". We picked him up on Friday afternoon and promised to return him Sunday evening.

It just so happened that Lynne and Tony's daughter Annette was getting married on that Saturday and we were invited to the evening reception. We arrived at the venue and almighty cheers rang out. Never has a wedding guest been made more welcome! We all had a great time but it was clear Matt had a long way to go before he was A1. He got very tired and his dancing, even in his wheelchair was not up to his usual standard. That first weekend was a learning curve. Matt was totally dependent on us but we had to respect that he also needed his own time and space. It was still so good to have him home.

So a new routine began. Intense physiotherapy throughout the week with Matt working as hard as humanly possible to get fit, then home again on Fridays until Sunday evening. During the week, weather permitting we often pushed him up to the local pub just for a change of scenery. When this happened we made a sign for his door "Gone to pub back by 10pm!" It meant staff and visitors knew where he was.

If we didn't go out to the pub and it was a warm evening we sat outside and Bonnie and Freddie were allowed to visit.

Eventually the great day, Friday 15th September came and he was discharged. The nurses gave him an enthusiastic send off and he donated the "Super soaker" to them for use on future inmates. He had to go back every Tuesday and Thursday for physiotherapy and obviously keep up his exercise regime at home.

As I was back at school Barry took him to all of these appointments. The feedback each time was good. Matt was making incredible progress, all that hard work was truly paying off. I shall never forget the first time I saw him take his tentative and unaided steps along the hospital corridor, the quality was so good. It was amazing to see him up on his feet again. He had attracted quite an audience all willing him on every step of the way. I of course was cheering through tears! But I wasn't the only one. His character stamp of determination had won through yet again!

Matt wrote a "Thank You" letter to all the staff and it made the front page of the Oaks Hospital Digest.

Matt:

Dear Oaks hospital staff,

You all must be a bunch of Angels for putting up with me for eight weeks. I know I'm not the easiest patient in the world but heh that's why you all love me (ha ha ha). I apologise to you all for being quiet and lacking a sense of humour, see it's the way I've been brought up, hopefully Lincoln Uni will teach me how to have a laugh!

Seriously now, thank you all for making this difficult time for me go by so quickly, you are all great!....(chatterboxes!) and thank goodness you were chatty cos talking to yourself gets a bit boring after a while, talking to the wall isn't much more interesting because they are nearly all plastered and are unable to put words together but then again I was half plastered for five weeks so I was in good company. Yes I've cracked but anyone would if they were being looked after by you lot with the fear of being squirted with water whilst lying helplessly in your sick bed. Then when you are able to move you are sent to the torture chamber where the physios unleash excruciating pain on you and when you beg for mercy they make you do more, especially if you ask for roast duck, (if this is being read by patients or future patients I am just kidding,) well except if you ask to eat duck then expect all your food to be rubbery! I have to say a big thank you to the merciless physios for my quick mobilization, your torture tactics made me work hard to get away from the torture.

To all the waitresses and waiters I would like to say thank you for serving me my meals with a smile, it made me uneasy because it made me wonder what you had put in it after all the grief I gave you and being fussy about my desserts (only joking!)

239

Thank you also to the cleaners for cleaning out my pit every day, I now know why you wore pegs on your noses.

Everyone who works at the Oaks really helped me get through this ordeal, with your caring personalities and your sense of humour. I have had such a laugh that it has made this stay an enjoyable one. It's great to have all this technology and drugs to make you better but they only do half the job, it may have made my hip better but you all made me feel better inside after a distressing year. So I would like to say a big THANK YOU TO YOU ALL

Love from
Matt Smith and family.XXX

Heartfelt praise that says it all. The next step along the road to university begins!

CHAPTER 56

PREPARING FOR UNIVERSITY

Once Matt was home from hospital there was so much to prepare for his new life at university. Our compensation claim, hopefully nearing its conclusion, was ever in the background. We had managed to finalise certain aspects, and get some projects underway. After some research and test-driving, the vehicle Matt had chosen which suited his needs most was a Chrysler Voyager, but even so it had to have some adaptations. The rear seats were removed so that folding ramps could be fitted, making life a lot easier to load and unload his electric wheelchair.

Our major concern was recruiting carers, not only for his personal needs but also to assist during the university day. On recommendation from our solicitors we appointed a Case Manager. This person would oversee the day to day running of his care plans, such as recruitment of carers, paying their wages and organizing timesheets etc. He also helped us formulate a job description to advertise and interview prospective candidates.

Matt had a very definite idea of the sort of person he wanted and the roles they would have to fulfill.

Practically, they had to be his "hands" but more importantly he needed a friend. He wanted someone who could not only provide practical help but also give him moral support as he carved out the next chapter of his life. The candidate would have to be very flexible as we couldn't as yet give them a defining role. A sense of humour and adventure was vital.

A young Australian called Rob answered our advert and was invited to our home for an interview. I can see him now, sitting in an armchair in our lounge. Bonnie plonked herself at his feet. She had clearly appointed herself the canine expert of the interviewing panel. Rob was obviously nervous but answered all of our questions well.

Bonnie was by now gazing up adoringly at him as he in turn dutifully rubbed her tummy. Rob hadn't realized that Bonnie was losing her coat and the area of navy blue carpet surrounding his chair was now a cloud of yellow fur.

He looked down in dismay and said "Oh no! I've stripped the Labrador!" Appointed on the spot.

Matt and Barry went up to Lincoln the following week to attend induction meetings and also to interview and hopefully recruit relief carers. Rob could not be expected to work 24 hours a day seven days a week. We had identified that Matt needed an assistant during the university day to help him get around the campus and take notes during lectures. They recruited a young man called Nathan, he came with excellent references and was also a Lincoln lad so he was invaluable at helping out with local knowledge.

During that week Matt attended various seminars and generally familiarized himself with his new surroundings. Matt's accommodation on campus was specially adapted for a wheelchair user, and there was also a carer's bedroom just across the corridor. It was all shaping up nicely. They both came home for Matt to have some final physiotherapy and to pack in readiness for university life.

Barry planned to spend the first week in Lincoln with Matt, so he could help him settle in and also help Rob and Nathan get to know each other and their new boss! Rob and Nathan had both done care work before but not quite like this so it was a learning curve for everyone.

Their input was going to be very important in working out their roles and times of shift change overs. Barry was going to be there during "Freshers"!!! (In fact he proved such a hit he was invited back for the next three years by popular demand, but that's another story!)

So the great day arrived, Sunday 8th October. The Voyager was loaded up and it was time to say our goodbyes! I can't really describe exactly how I felt as Nikki and I stood on the drive to wave them off.

Matt had made me promise not to cry and I did my level best to oblige. Our little lad was now at the beginning of an exciting new life, a life in which I was no longer to be the broker of all his needs. The apron strings were finally cut. His own determination and wicked sense of humour had got him to this stage. The achievement was enormous.

What happens next would be solely down to Matt. I leave you with some of Barry's memories of those first "Lincoln" days!

At last escaped; made it to Lincoln University and some memorable "Fresher's" nights out. October 2000

BARRY:

LINCOLN 2000

We had purchased a Chrysler Voyager people carrier for Matt and had ramps installed for his wheelchair. It was a lovely vehicle, comfortable and great to drive. So, onto our arrival at Lincoln University for Matt to begin his studies for a BA Hons degree in Journalism and English.

We got to Matt's halls of residence early on arrivals day Sunday 17th September 2000. There was no shortage of very friendly and willing helpers (all student volunteers). Matt was to be on the ground floor of one of the many recently constructed 3 storey halls of residence buildings situated within 400 metres of the University Campus. There were eight other student rooms in his apartment, one of which was to be a carer's room. All rooms had ensuite facilities and the students shared a communal kitchen and lounge/dining living area. Matt's room was fully adapted with wet room etc.

Gradually throughout this first day Matt's new flat-mates arrived and initially it was definitely a case of Oh! A disabled flat mate who they could hardly understand and his middle aged dad! Whoopee! In the main this attitude didn't last very long! By evening all of the students in the flat had arrived bar one and having unloaded their belongings were either out exploring or in their rooms. I was in the carer's room and Matt was in the lounge area. It was probably about 8pm and I heard conversation coming from the lounge involving Matt and what sounded like a young lady's voice. The carer's and Matt's rooms were both next door to the communal area. I was just on the verge of going through to join Matt; thinking he would need me to translate for him, when I suddenly thought that Matt did seem to be getting on okay thank you very much, so I stayed where I was!

Some half an hour later Matt called me to join him and he introduced me to his new friend Ginny, a very attractive dark haired young lady! She had literally only just arrived all the way from Cumbria a short while before she met Matt. From that very first meeting Ginny and Matt had hit it off and she had no problem understanding what Matt was saying! They are still good friends to this day.

In addition to Matt having a new friend and ally who could understand him; Ginny's arrival seemed to give him some "Street Cred" with his other fellow flatmates. I felt that they looked at Matt in a slightly different light than when first meeting him.

The Monday was spent setting up Matt's PC etc. and familiarizing ourselves with his new environs. The Students Union Volunteers were very much in evidence and were actively recruiting the "New Intake" for the first evening activities for the coming night, which was the beginning of Freshers Week! In the day time on that first week there was the usual enrolment, inductions and seminars. There were also initial lectures in English and Journalism. Additionally, in Matt's case we had numerous meetings with the Disabled Student Support people. Also meetings with private care agency staff with a view to finding local carers/assistants to help Matt in an ongoing role.

On the Tuesday Matt's Uncle Peter and Aunty Jean from Hull paid us a visit in the afternoon with Matt's cousin Alvin, their son. I must confess that when I eventually left Matt on his own in Lincoln with his carers that it was very re-assuring that Jean, Peter and Alvin were less than fifty miles away!   Matt's first social venture was on the Sunday evening of our arrival. A disco was held in the Atrium of the main campus building. To this day I still can't hear S Club 7's "Reach for the stars" without being immediately transported back to that first night and remembering all the young students

245

including Matt dancing to that particular number. A few drinks definitely got sunk that evening! That first night Matt met many people from the S.U. who went on to become very good friends and one in particular, Cate, who became his best mate!

The Atrium had a refectory situated just across the way and if we were up early enough in the mornings a very good full English breakfast could be had!!

There were constant visits to Matt's flat by S.U. volunteers who were drumming up support for the events taking place that evening which inevitably involved a drinking function! The first organized night on the Monday was a Pub Crawl. This involved numerous pubs and bars which included; The Varsity Bar, The Lion and Snake, The Hogshead (Shed) and Vodka Revolution where I tasted my first Mississippi Mudslide. Each of the bars had various "Treats" lined up for the "Freshers". Some had shots of this or that and others had different challenges but invariably all involved the consumption of alcohol.

Old Lincoln stands atop a very large hill; in fact on the edge of the Wolds which stretch virtually all the way to Skegness about forty miles away.

The main route up the old part where the Cathedral and Castle are situated, along with loads of old pubs, is a steep Hill. So steep in fact that the S.U. organized shuttle buses to transport the revellers between Brayford Campus and surrounding pubs to the top and visa versa.

Matt and I did get separated on more than one occasion during that first week on our nighttime outings. He would go one way and I would go another; "independence for both of us!" On one of these excursions it took me about two hours to catch up with Matt who was drinking with some of his new found friends in a pub "down the hill".

I was with three of his flat-mates who just happened to be young ladies; Lisa, Ginny and Lindsey. We had a few drinks in the VK Revolution bar and then wandered down to find Matt. When we got to the pub that he was in we thought it would be a good laugh if I pretended to be Paralytic!! So we entered said pub with me propped up by "a young lady on either side of me". To this day Matt insists that I really was paralytic, but I know the truth!

There were fancy dress themed nights; one of which was a casino night requiring formal wear. Matt and I looked pretty cool dudes and in my white D.J. I went as Basildon; "Basildon Bond!" One night later in the week cousin Alvin came over from Hull and stayed the night. This meant that I was able to leave Matt to continue his night out with Alvin whilst I returned to the flat for an early night. I think I got to bed at about 1am!

I have to say that Matt wasn't an early riser but during the daytime we did have to interview prospective carers/note takers to supplement his main live-in carer Rob, a gay Australian Buddhist and a great guy. The successful applicant for the main support worker alongside Rob was a young local man called Nathan (yet another Man U supporter). I don't know whether it influenced Matt's decision to employ him. We also engaged a couple of students on a casual as and when basis. It suited them because they needed the money and us because it gave Matt some back up.

Going back to carer Rob reminds me of the one and only time that I have ever phoned the Colchester "Gay Switchboard". Matt and Rob were coming home for a weekend and Matt wanted Rob to have some recreational time off. Matt thought it would be helpful if we could tell Rob which pubs were the gay pubs in Colchester. I duly rang the Gay Switchboard and a pleasant young man answered. I explained that I wanted to know which pubs were gay or gay friendly. I then said that this information wasn't for me (in a very deep masculine voice); but for my son's friend! He didn't say a word out of place to me but I could hear him thinking "yes of course you're ringing on someone elses behalf!!" I then compounded matters by asking if a particular pub in town that I'd heard was a gay pub actually was. He replied that he hadn't actually heard that it was but would add it to his list to try out!

I've had stick about this phone call for years; although apparently Rob did have a couple of evenings in town which he said he thoroughly enjoyed! Sadly Matt lost Rob as a carer when he went on a Buddhist retreat in Scotland and broke his back tobogganing! We got the call informing us of this on New Years day 2001. Happy New Year to everyone! I feel that Matt got the very best shot at independence at Lincoln Uni as a result of Wendy and me being able to let go and allow him to experience life without us continually looking over his shoulder. Although I have to confess it was not that easy to let him make his own mistakes at times.

EPILOGUE

Why have I written this book?

So many reasons spring to mind it's difficult to evaluate them.

Primarily because I suppose selfishly it's a valuable story to share.

It's my account of the trials, tribulations and triumphs that have beset an "impaired" child together with the impact on their family and friends.

Our own very personal experiences of going through life coping with not only the difficulties but more importantly the successes that came along may be of benefit to other families in similar circumstances.

Mostly however I wanted to share and celebrate the achievements no matter how great or small.

Matt has touched many lives, some with admiration others with anger but very rarely with indifference. All parents and guardians are proud of their children, even more so if life's dice is loaded against them.

Matt's life has shaped and influenced the people that are Barry, Wendy and Nikki Smith.

It would be arrogant and unrealistic to suppose we are better people because of this. I do however like to think we are more enlightened, tolerant and certainly able to find the funny side of life.

If our story can help or inspire other families then it has been a worthwhile exercise. Especially if the comedy made you smile.

I hope with all my heart Matt will one day write the sequel.

UPDATE 2015

As in all families we have had our family bereavements. It is so hard especially when those folk have given so much. In 2003 we said goodbye to our lovely Peter. Happily he was able to walk daughter Helen down the aisle before his illness overtook him. He has left an enormous hole in our family.

Grandma passed away at the grand age of 98. She was still the Matriarch of our family and living independently. Indomitable and irreplaceable!

In 2011 our greatest supporter, Barry's brother Alan, who was also his best friend, died. He lost a long and incredibly brave fight. He has provided so many happy memories to keep in the treasure box.

MATT

The Health Authority admitted liability and made an 'Out of court' settlement. He graduated from Lincoln University with a very creditable 2.2 degree in English and Journalism

Lincoln is now 'home' to Matt and he leads a busy life doing some charity and advocacy work. He has appeared on BBC's Look North when he took up the cudgels to defend disabled people having extra time for parking in public car parks.

His latest passion is power chair football and he recently took and passed his coaching badge. Matt is a great exponent of the game and plays for Nottingham Forest.

A team of carers work with Matt and he enjoys a great quality of life.

NIKKI

In December 2012 we gained a lovely son-in-law Ben. Nikki graduated from the University of East Anglia in June 2013 as Doctor Burnand. Her first two years as doctor were spent in Aberdeen and Inverness but Nikki and Ben are now following a dream of living and working in New Zealand. They manage to keep in close contact with the rest of us through the wonders of Skype.

BARRY

Barry has semi-retired from the Financial Industry and spends a lot of time on the golf course. He is also chairman of the Former Players Association of Colchester United.

WENDY

I have also semi-retired but am still working three days a week as a learning support assistant at Market Field School. I still love working at a very special school with equally special children.

When I'm not working I enjoy Badminton, cooking, reading, gardening and walking our dog Monty. The famous footballer and the Mayor's daughter are still together!